GOSPEL SHAPED

LIVING

Leader's Guide

GOSPEL SHAPED

LIVING

Vermon Pierre

 THE GOSPEL
COALITION

 **the goodbook**
COMPANY

Gospel Shaped Living Leader's Guide
© The Gospel Coalition / The Good Book Company 2015

Published by:
The Good Book Company
Tel (US): 866 244 2165
Tel (UK): 0333 123 0880
Email (US): info@thegoodbook.com
Email (UK): info@thegoodbook.co.uk

Websites:
North America: www.thegoodbook.com
UK: www.thegoodbook.co.uk
Australia: www.thegoodbook.com.au
New Zealand: www.thegoodbook.co.nz

ISBN: 9781909919266 Printed in the US

PRODUCTION TEAM:

AUTHOR:
Vermon Pierre

**SERIES EDITOR FOR
THE GOSPEL COALITION:**
Collin Hansen

**SERIES EDITOR FOR
THE GOOD BOOK COMPANY:**
Tim Thornborough

**MAIN TEACHING SESSION
DISCUSSIONS:** Alison Mitchell

DAILY DEVOTIONALS:
Carl Laferton

BIBLE STUDIES:
Tim Thornborough

EDITORIAL ASSISTANTS:
Jeff Robinson (TGC), Rachel Jones (TGBC)

VIDEO EDITOR:
Phil Grout

PROJECT ADMINISTRATOR:
Jackie Moralee

EXECUTIVE PRODUCER:
Brad Byrd

DESIGN:
André Parker

CONTENTS

PREFACE

GROWING A GOSPEL SHAPED CHURCH

The Gospel Coalition is a group of pastors and churches in the Reformed heritage who delight in the truth and power of the gospel, and who want the gospel of Christ crucified and resurrected to lie at the center of all we cherish, preach and teach.

We want churches called into existence by the gospel to be shaped by the gospel in their everyday life.

Through our fellowship, conferences, and online and printed media, we have sought to encourage pastors and church leaders to calibrate their lives around what is of first importance—the gospel of Christ. In these resources, we want to provide those same pastors with the tools to excite and equip church members with this mindset.

In our foundation documents, we identified five areas that should mark the lives of believers in a local fellowship:

1. Empowered corporate worship
2. Evangelistic effectiveness
3. Counter-cultural community
4. The integration of faith and work
5. The doing of justice and mercy

We believe that a church utterly committed to winsome and theologically substantial expository preaching, and that lives out the gospel in these areas, will display its commitment to dynamic evangelism, apologetics, and church planting. These gospel-shaped churches will emphasize repentance, personal renewal, holiness, and the wonderful life of the church as the body of Christ. At the same time, there will be engagement with the social structures of ordinary people, and cultural engagement with art, business, scholarship and government. The church will be characterized by firm devotion to the truth on the one hand, and by transparent compassion on the other.

The Gospel Coalition believes in the priority of the local church, and that the local church is the best place to discuss these five ministry drivers and decide how to integrate them into life and mission. So, while being clear on the biblical principles, these resources give space to consider what a genuine expression of a gospel-shaped church looks like for you in the place where God has put you, and with the people he has gathered into fellowship with you.

Through formal teaching sessions, daily Bible devotionals, group Bible studies and the regular preaching ministry, it is our hope and prayer that congregations will grow into maturity, and so honor and glorify our great God and Savior.

Don Carson
President

Tim Keller
Vice President

 # INTRODUCTION

We have become used to a lot of things today—things we have come to accept as a normal part of living in our world.

We accept that conflict is just a part of daily life; and we accept that conflict between people will inevitably lead to division and dysfunction. We accept that people will be motivated by selfishness, and make choices based on their needs before considering the needs of others. We accept that people will tell lies and distort the truth to their own advantage. We accept that life will be a struggle, and will end in suffering and death. We have accepted that nasty is normal.

Yet at the same time, everyone instinctively senses that this is *just not right*. That life doesn't have to be this way; that things ought to be different. This may be normal life, but it isn't optimal life.

Christians are people who have discovered that something incredible has happened—something that broke through the walls built up around what we're used to and what our world accepts as normal. This "something" is that Jesus Christ rose from the dead. And because he rose, everything is different. Change, forgiveness and new life are now possible. A crack of light has broken into the darkness of the world. Division, dysfunction, selfishness and death do not have to be the final answer. Rather, by faith in Christ, we can now live the life of Christ.

And when Christians who are gathered together as the church live out this life within the world, they become a truly "counter-cultural community"—a community that still lives within the culture, but now shines with the light of a new culture, one shaped by and grounded in the gospel of Jesus Christ.

The Gospel Coalition has included this statement in their Theological Vision for Ministry, entitled "Counter-cultural community." It begins:

> *Because the gospel removes both fear and pride, people should get along*
> *inside the church who could never get along outside. Because it points us to a*
> *man who died for his enemies, the gospel creates relationships of service rather*

than of selfishness. Because the gospel calls us to holiness, the people of God live in loving bonds of mutual accountability and discipline. Thus the gospel creates a human community radically different from any society around it.[1]

In this curriculum we will think through what it means for a church to be a counter-cultural community within the world. We won't do that by thinking primarily about culture, style or gimmicks—but about the gospel. We will see some of the principal ways in which a church that is being shaped by the gospel will live in stark contrast to the world around us; and how this will set it both at odds with its society, and yet also be strangely attractive to those in that society.

For example, what does it mean for the church to show unity in contrast to worldly divisions? What impact will it have when a self-centered world sees a church community that is full of sacrificial love and generosity? How can Christians hold to and speak out about truth in a way that is loving?

You might be unsettled as you work through this material and see significant areas where you and your church are still too much like the world, or too distant from the world. Don't give up or try to avoid what the Lord needs to reveal within you and your church. Instead, prayerfully work through these sessions with the happy and humble confidence that God wants to fill you even more with "the light of the gospel of the glory of Christ" (2 Corinthians 4:4). Trust that as this happens, many of the people you know and interact with day by day will begin to walk away from the darkness of sin and be drawn toward the light of the gospel.

Vermon Pierre

---

1 You can read the full text of the statement on page 158 of the Handbook.

MAKING THE MOST OF
GOSPEL SHAPED
CHURCH

WHAT GOSPEL SHAPED CHURCH WILL DO FOR YOU

God is in the business of changing people and changing churches. He always does that through his gospel.

Through the gospel he changed us from his enemies to his friends, and through the gospel he brought us into a new family to care for each other and to do his will in the world. The gospel brings life and creates churches.

But the gospel of Jesus, God's Son, our Savior and Lord, isn't merely what begins our Christian life and forms new churches. It is the pattern, and provides the impetus, for all that follows. So Paul wrote to the Colossian church:

> Therefore, as you received Christ Jesus the Lord, so walk in him, rooted and built up in him and established in the faith, just as you were taught, abounding in thanksgiving (Colossians 2:6-7).

"As you received … so walk…" In other words, the secret of growing as a Christian is to continue to reflect upon and build your life on the gospel of the lordship of Jesus Christ. And the secret of growing as a church is to let the gospel inform and energize every single aspect of a church's life, both in what you do and how you do it, from your sermons to young mothers' groups; from your budget decisions and your pastoral care to your buildings maintenance and church bulletins.

Letting the gospel shape a church requires the whole church to be shaped by the gospel. To be, and become, gospel shaped is not a task merely for the senior pastor, or the staff team, or the board of elders. It is something that happens as every member considers the way in which the gospel should continue to shape their walk, and the life of their church.

That is the conviction that lies behind this series of five resources from The Gospel

Coalition. It will invite your church members to be part of the way in which you shape your church according to the unchanging gospel, in your particular culture and circumstances. It will excite and equip your whole church to be gospel shaped. It will envision you together, from senior church staff to your newest believer. It will enable you all to own the vision of a gospel-shaped church, striving to teach that gospel to one another and to reach your community with that gospel. As you continue to work out together the implications of the gospel that has saved us, you will be guided into Christian maturity in every area of your lives, both personal and corporate.

This resource is for all kinds of churches: large and small; urban and rural; new plants and long-established congregations; all denominations and none. It is for any congregation that has been given life by the gospel and wants to put the gospel at the center of its life.

You can use the five tracks in any order you like—and you can use as many or as few of them as you wish. If you think your church is lacking in one particular area, it will always be helpful to focus on that for a season. But it is our hope that you will plan to run all five parts of the curriculum with your church—perhaps over a 3- or 4-year time frame. Some tracks may be more like revision and confirmation that you are working well in those areas. Others will open up new areas of service and change that you need to reflect upon. But together they will help you grow into an organic maturity as you reflect on the implications of the gospel in every area of life.

HOW TO MAKE THE MOST OF THIS CURRICULUM

Because the gospel, as it is articulated in the pages of the Bible, should be the foundation of everything we do, this resource is designed to work best if a congregation gives itself over to exploring the themes together as a whole. That means shaping the whole of church life for a season around the theme. The overall aim is to get the DNA of the gospel into the DNA of your church life, structures, practices and people.

So it is vitally important that you involve as many people in your congregation as possible in the process, so that there is a sense that this is a journey that the whole church has embarked upon together. The more you immerse yourselves in this material, the more you will get from it. But equally, all churches are different, and so this material is flexible enough to fit any and every church program and structure—see page 24 for more details.

Here are some other suggestions for how to make the most of this material.

PREPARE
Work through the material in outline with your leadership team and decide which elements best fit where. Will you use the sermon suggestions, or develop a series of your own? Will you teach through the main sessions in Sunday School, or in midweek groups? Will you use the teaching DVD, or give your own talks?

Think about some of the likely pressure points this discussion will create in your congregation. How will you handle in a constructive way any differences of opinion that come out of this? Decide together how you will handle feedback. There will be many opportunities for congregation members to express their ideas and thoughts, and as you invite them to think about your church's life, they will have many suggestions. It will be overwhelming to have everyone emailing or calling the Senior Pastor; but it will be very frustrating if church members feel they are not truly being listened to, and that nothing will really change. So organize a system of feedback from group-discussion leaders and Bible-study leaders; make clear which member of senior staff will collect that feedback; and schedule time as a staff team to listen to your members' thoughts, and pray about and consider them.

There is an online feedback form that could be distributed and used to round off the whole track with your congregation.

PROMOTE

Encourage your congregation to buy into the process by promoting it regularly and building anticipation. Show the trailer at all your church meetings and distribute your own customized version of the bulletin insert (download from www.gospelshapedchurch.org).

Embarking on this course together should be a big deal. Make sure your congregation knows what it might mean for them, and what an opportunity it represents in the life of your whole church; and make sure it sounds like an exciting adventure in faith.

Do involve the whole church. Younger children may not be able to grasp the implications of some things, but certainly those who teach and encourage children of 11 and upwards will be able to adapt the material and outlines here to something that is age appropriate.

PRAY

Pray as a leadership team that the Lord would lead you all into new, exciting ways of serving him.

Encourage the congregation to pray. There are plenty of prompts in the material for this to happen, but do pray at your regular meetings for the Lord's help and guidance as you study, think and discuss together. Building in regular prayer times will help your congregation move together as a fellowship. Prayer connects us to God, but it also connects us to each other, as we address our Father together. And our God "is able to do far more abundantly than all that we ask or think" (Ephesians 3:20) as his people ask him to enable them to grasp, and be shaped by, the love of Christ that is shown to us in his gospel.

FOUR WAYS TO MAKE (OR BREAK) THIS PROCESS

1. BE OPEN TO CHANGE AS A CHURCH

As churches that love the gospel, we should always be reforming to live more and more in line with that gospel. Change isn't always easy, and is often sacrificial; but it is exciting, and part of the way in which we obey our Lord. Approach this exploration of *Gospel Shaped Living* by encouraging your church to be willing to change where needed.

2. BE OPEN TO CHANGE YOURSELF

This curriculum will lead every member to think hard about how the gospel should shape, and in some ways re-shape, your church. You are giving them permission to suggest making changes. As a leader, giving such permission is both exciting and intimidating. It will *make* your course if you enter it as a leadership excited to see how your church may change and how you may be challenged. It will *break* it if you approach it hoping or expecting that your members will simply agree in every way with what you have already decided.

3. DISCUSS GRACIOUSLY

Keep talking about grace and community. Church is about serving others and giving up "my" own wants, not about meeting "my" own social preferences and musical tastes. Encourage your membership to pursue discussions that are positive, open and non-judgmental, and to be able to disagree lovingly and consider others' feelings before their own, rather than seeking always to "win." Model gospel grace in the way you talk about the gospel of grace.

4. REMEMBER WHO IS IN CHARGE

Jesus Christ is Lord of your church—not the leadership, the elders or the membership. So this whole process needs to be bathed in a prayerful sense of commitment to follow him, and to depend on his strength and guidance for any change his Spirit is prompting. Keep reminding your church that this process is not about becoming the church they want, but the one your Lord wants.

HOW TO USE
GOSPEL SHAPED
LIVING

HOW TO USE GOSPEL SHAPED LIVING

Gospel Shaped Living is designed to be a flexible resource to fit a wide variety of church settings. The **Main Teaching Session** is the core of the curriculum—the other components grow out of this. The more elements you use, the greater the benefit will be to your church.

The elements of this course are:

- **MAIN TEACHING SESSION** with DVD or talk, and discussion (core)
- **PERSONAL DEVOTIONALS** (recommended)
- **GROUP BIBLE STUDY** (recommended)
- **PERSONAL JOURNAL** (optional)
- **SERMON SERIES** (suggested passages given)

Each church member will need a copy of the *Gospel Shaped Living Handbook*. This contains everything they need to take part in the course, including the discussion questions for the **Main Teaching Session**, **Personal Devotionals**, and the **Group Bible Study**. There's also space to make notes during the sermon, and a **Personal Journal** to keep a record of the things they have been learning.

Each person who will be leading a group discussion, either in the **Main Teaching Session** or the **Group Bible Study**, will need a copy of the *Gospel Shaped Living Leader's Guide*. This includes leader's notes to help them guide a small group through the discussion or Bible-study questions, and other resources to give more background and detail. In the Leader's Guide, all the instructions, questions, comments, prayer points etc. that also appear in the Handbook are in **bold text**.

Further copies of the *Handbook* and *Leader's Guide* are available from **WWW.GOSPELSHAPEDCHURCH.ORG/LIVING**

A FLEXIBLE CURRICULUM

Gospel Shaped Living is designed to be a flexible resource. You may be able to give your whole church over to working through it. If so, a typical week might look like this:

SUNDAY
- Adult Sunday school: **Main Teaching Session** using DVD or live talk (talk outline given in *Leader's Guide*)
- Morning service: **Sermon** based on main theme (suggested Bible passages given in the *Leader's Guide*)

MIDWEEK
- Small groups work through the **Group Bible Study**

CHURCH MEMBERS
- Use the **Personal Devotionals** from Monday to Saturday
- Use the **Personal Journal** to record their thoughts, questions and ideas about things they've been learning throughout the week

Or, if you choose to use the curriculum on a midweek basis, it may be like this:

MIDWEEK
- Small groups work through the **Main Teaching Session** using the DVD

CHURCH MEMBERS
- Use the **Personal Devotionals** from Monday to Saturday
- Use the **Personal Journal** to record their thoughts, questions and ideas about things they've been learning throughout the week

Or you can use the components in any other way that suits your church practice.

HOW TO USE EACH ELEMENT

These sample pages from the *Gospel Shaped Living Handbook* show the different elements of the curriculum.

All of the material in this curriculum quotes from and is based on the ESV Bible.

MAIN TEACHING SESSION
- 60 minutes
- Choose between DVD or live talk
- Discussion questions to help group members discuss the DVD/talk and apply it to their own lives and their church
- Guidance for answering the questions is given in the *Leader's Guide*
- Suggestions for praying together

This is the core of the curriculum. It can be run using the *Gospel Shaped Living DVD*, or by giving a live talk. A summary of the talk is included in the *Leader's Guide* (see page 34 for an example). A full editable script can also be downloaded from **www.gospelshapedchurch.org/living/talks**.

In each session, the DVD/talk is split into either two or three sections, each followed by some discussion questions. At the end of the session there are suggestions to help the group pray specifically for each other.

The discussion questions are designed to help church members unpack the teaching they have heard and apply it to their own lives and to the church as a whole. There are not necessarily right and wrong answers to some of the questions, as this will often depend on the context of your own church. Let group members discuss these openly, and apply them to their own situation.

Keep the discussion groups the same each week if possible, with the same leader (who will need a copy of this *Leader's Guide*) for each group, so that relationships are deepened and the discussions can build on those of previous sessions.

PERSONAL DEVOTIONALS

- Six devotionals with each session
- Designed to be started the day after the main teaching session
- Linked with the theme for each teaching session, but based on different Bible passages
- Help church members dig more deeply into the theme on a daily basis

Each session is followed by six personal devotionals that build on the main theme. They are ideal for church members to use between sessions. For example, if you have the main teaching session on a Sunday, church members can then use the devotionals from Monday to Saturday.

These short devotionals can be used in addition to any regular personal Bible study being done by church members. They would also form a useful introduction for anyone trying out personal Bible reading for the first time.

As well as being in the group member's **Handbook**, the personal devotionals are available for a small fee on the Explore Bible Devotional app. This can be downloaded from the iTunes App Store or Google Play (search for "Explore Bible Devotional"). Select "Gospel Shaped Living" from the app's download menu.

PERSONAL JOURNAL

- A useful place for church members to note down what they have been learning throughout the week, and any questions they may have

SERMON NOTES

- If the Sunday sermon series is running as part of **Gospel Shaped Living**, this is a helpful place to make notes

GROUP BIBLE STUDY

- 40 – 50 minutes
- An ideal way for small groups to build on what they have been learning in the main teaching
- Uses a different Bible passage from the DVD/talk
- Suggested answers to the questions are given in the *Leader's Guide*

This study is ideal for a home group or other group to work through together. It builds on the theme covered by the main teaching session, but is based on a different Bible passage. You can see the passages and themes listed in the grid on pages 28-29.

If possible, give 40 – 50 minutes for the Bible study. However, it can be covered in 30 minutes if necessary, and if you keep a close eye on time. If your church is not using the Bible studies as part of a regular group, they would also be suitable for individuals to do on their own or in a pair if they want to do some further study on the themes being looked at in the course.

SERMON SUGGESTIONS

The *Leader's Guide* gives a choice of three sermon suggestions to tie in with each session:

- A passage that is used in the main teaching session (DVD or live talk)
- The Bible reading that is being studied in the Group Bible Study that week
- A third passage that is not being used elsewhere, but that picks up on the same themes. This is the passage that is listed in the overview grid on pages 28-29.

FURTHER READING

At the end of each session in the *Leader's Guide* you will find a page of suggestions for further reading. This gives ideas for books, articles, blog posts, videos, etc. that relate to the session, together with some quotes that you might use in sermons, discussion groups and conversations. Some of these may be helpful in your preparation, as well as helping any group members who want to think more deeply about the topic they've been discussing.

CURRICULUM OUTLINE AT A GLANCE

SESSION	MAIN TEACHING (DVD/TALK)	PERSONAL DEVOTIONS	GROUP BIBLE STUDY	SERMON*
1 Your church: a light in the darkness	God's church is to be a light *in* the darkness and a light *for* the darkness. Based on **Matthew 5:14-16** and **1 Peter 2:9-10**.	**1 Peter 2:9-10**, looking back to the Old Testament to see a breathtaking description of who your church is.	**Luke 5:27-32** The Lord Jesus models for us what it is to be a light in and for the darkness.	REV 1:9-20
2 A united church in a divided world	God's people are called to be united. How can we achieve this when we are a collection of selfish sinners? Based on **Ephesians 2:11-18**.	How can we, as individual church members, positively foster unity in our churches? **Romans 12:9-21**.	**Genesis 11:1-9** and **Acts 2:1-13** Looking at how unity is part of the whole Bible story, and the implications for our unity as a local church.	1 COR 12:12-31
3 A serving church in a selfish world	The way to be great in the kingdom of God is to be a servant of all. Based on **Matthew 20:20-28**.	Six Gospel passages that reveal how Jesus spent his time on earth. **Luke 7, 8, 12, 13, 14, 21 and 22**.	**Philippians 2** Looking at some practical examples of sacrificial service in action.	JOHN 13:1-17
4 A generous church in a stingy world	How does and how should the gospel shape our finances? How can the church stand out as "an island of generosity" in a stingy world? Based on **2 Corinthians 8:1-9**.	Focusing on our wallets as we work through **2 Corinthians 8 – 9**.	**Luke 19:1-10** Reinforcing the challenge to be people characterized by generous grace.	PROV 19:17; 21:13; 30:7-9

	SESSION	MAIN TEACHING (DVD/TALK)	PERSONAL DEVOTIONS	GROUP BIBLE STUDY	SERMON*
5	A truthful church in a confused world	This session calls us back to a robust trust in God's truth, revealed in his Son. Various passages including **John 1**, **John 14** and **Ephesians 4**.	Taking a close look at Paul's teaching on love, obedience, sex and relationships in **1 Thessalonians 4:1-12**.	**1 Thessalonians 2:1-12** Considering the hostility we will face when we speak the truth, and how we can model the love and grace of Christ as we maintain a faithful witness.	JOHN 4:1-30
6	A joyful church in a suffering world	How is it possible to have joy in the midst of suffering? Based on the book of **Habakkuk**.	**Romans 8:1-39**, looking at six great truths we can cling onto when suffering.	**Hebrews 11 and 12** Suffering is "normal" for Christians. So what will help us maintain our trust in God?	1 PETER 1:3-9
7	How to be the church in the world	We are not left alone to be a light in a dark world. God's Spirit works in, through and around us to make it possible. Based on **Galatians 5 – 6**.	Studying the church in **Acts** to see how we can shine brightly in the world.	**Galatians 5:25 – 6:10** What will it mean for us to grow in Christ-likeness, as we seek to burn brighter as a light in the world?	MATTHEW 5:14-16

* NOTE: The *Leader's Guide* gives three sermon suggestions to tie in with each session. The first picks up a passage from the Main Teaching Session; the second uses the passage from the Group Bible Study; and the third is a new passage, linked with the theme but not used elsewhere in the session. This third passage is the one listed here.

DOWNLOADS

In addition to the material in this *Leader's Guide*, there are a number of extra downloadable resources and enhancements. You will find all of them listed under the Living track at **www.gospelshapedchurch.org** and on The Good Book Company's website: **www.thegoodbook.com/gsc**.

- **DIGITAL DOWNLOAD OF DVD MATERIAL.** If you have already bought a DVD as part of the *Leader's Kit*, you will have access to a single HD download of the material using the code on the download card. If you want to download additional digital copies, in SD or HD, these can be purchased from The Good Book Company website: **www.thegoodbook.com/gsc**.

- **DVD TRAILERS.** Trailers and promotional pieces for the series as a whole and for the individual tracks can be downloaded for free. Use these trailers to excite your church about being involved in *Gospel Shaped Church*.

- **TALK TRANSCRIPTS.** We're conscious that for some churches and situations, it may be better to deliver your own talk for the main session so that it can be tailored specifically to your people and context. You can download the talk transcript as both a PDF and as an editable Word document.

- **FEEDBACK FORMS.** Because *Gospel Shaped Church* is designed as a whole-church exploration, it's important that you think through carefully how you will handle suggestions and feedback. There's some guidance for that on pages 17-18. We've provided a downloadable feedback form that you can use as part of the way in which you end your time using the resource. Simply print it and distribute it to your church membership to gather their thoughts and ideas, and to get a sense of the issues you may want to focus on for the future. In addition, there are also fully editable versions of this feedback form so that you can create your own customized sheet that works effectively for the way in which you have used this material, and which suits your church membership. Alternatively, you could use the questions to create your own online feedback form with Google Forms or some other software, to make collecting and collating information easier.

- **RESOURCE LIST.** For each session in this *Leader's Guide* we have included a list of resources that will help you in your preparation for sermons, discussions, Bible studies and other conversations. On the *Gospel Shaped Church* website, you will find an up-to-date list of resources, plus a shorter downloadable list that you might consider giving to church members to supplement their own reading and thinking.

- **BULLETIN TEMPLATES.** Enclosed with the *Leader's Kit* is a sample of a bulletin-insert design to promote the Living track to your church. You can download a printable PDF of the design from the *Gospel Shaped Church* website to add your own details, and to print and distribute to your congregation.

- **OTHER PROMOTIONAL MATERIAL.** Editable powerpoint slides and other promotional material to use.

 WWW.GOSPELSHAPEDCHURCH.ORG/LIVING

 WWW.THEGOODBOOK.COM/GSC/LIVING

SESSION 1:

YOUR CHURCH: A LIGHT IN THE DARKNESS

BOTH INSIDE AND OUTSIDE THE CHURCH, THERE ARE MANY DIFFERENT VIEWS OF WHAT A CHURCH ACTUALLY IS. IN THIS INTRODUCTORY SESSION, YOU'LL DISCOVER HOW GOD'S CHURCH IS MADE UP OF UNIQUE PEOPLE, WITH A UNIQUE PURPOSE. AND YOU'LL BEGIN TO SEE WHY GOD HAS PUT YOU IN YOUR CHURCH, AND WHY HE HAS PUT YOUR CHURCH WHERE HE HAS.

TALK OUTLINE

1.1 • The church: An irrelevant old-folks' home? A pit of hypocritical vipers? Ignorant judgmental weirdos? Some accusations are true, but they certainly shouldn't be!

• **WHAT IS THE CHURCH?** *Matthew 5:14-16*
  • Lots of attitudes toward church focus on *us*—they treat church as a commodity to be consumed to meet our needs. *Give examples of what these attitudes look like.*
  • Instead, we are people who "shine" in a dark world—a bright, shining community with a mission to give itself for the benefit of a world trapped in spiritual gloom.
  • The church is a light *for* the world: **different** than the world, but not **separate**.

1.2 • **A UNIQUE PEOPLE** *1 Peter 2:9-10*
  • We were once living in darkness, until we heard the good news about Jesus. Now we've been made into a "**chosen race**": a whole new category of human being.
  • Although on the surface we may have little in common, the church is the only community of relationships which will last forever!
  • We've all received "spiritual welfare" and have been adopted into God's family (v 10): this should form the basis of our identity forever.
  • We are to be **holy** (v 9), or "set apart." We are to live in a way that sets us apart from the dominant culture.

1.3 • **A UNIQUE PURPOSE**
  • The church is "a royal priesthood" (v 9). Like OT priests, Christians have direct access to God; we're called to **represent** God as King to the rest of the world.
  • The purpose of the church is to live out and proclaim the gospel of Jesus Christ. This is best understood as something the church *is*, not something it *does*. Something of the beauty of Christ can even be seen in our everyday activities.
  • The world accepts a substandard version of humanity; but in Jesus, we see true humanity.

• **CONCLUSION:** As we own our identity as a unique and chosen people, we can prayerfully expect God to call people into the goodness of the light of his grace.

You can download a full transcript of these talks at
WWW.GOSPELSHAPEDCHURCH.ORG/LIVING/TALKS

YOUR CHURCH: A LIGHT IN THE DARKNESS

* *Ask the group members to turn to Session 1 on page 13 of the Handbook.*

Discuss

What do people who don't go to church think of Christians and the church?

This starter question is to get people thinking and talking about the concept of church, and how the church is viewed by the wider world. Ask people to give just one-word answers—this will keep the discussion short.

▶ **WATCH DVD 1.1** (6 min 16 sec) **OR DELIVER TALK 1.1** (see page 34)

* *Encourage the group to make notes as they watch the DVD or listen to the talk. There is space for notes on page 15 of the Handbook.*

Discuss

How do people treat the church as consumers? Do you ever find yourself doing this?

Treating the church as a consumer means focusing on what we get out of church, rather than what we can give. Examples include: just turning up at the beginning of a service expecting everything to be set up and ready; choosing a church on the basis of the music, the length (or brevity!) of the sermon, the kind of people in the congregation, etc; being vocal about complaints but not grateful when things go well.

Give the group an opportunity to consider whether this sometimes applies to their own view of church. The aim isn't that individuals start to feel guilty about

35

this, but that they start to think about areas they may want to change as a result of working through this curriculum together.

What unhelpful things does this lead to? What are people missing out on who treat their Christian faith in this way?

If we just think as consumers, this can mean we assess everything in terms of how well it suits our own needs (or those of our family). This leads to a church that works well for people who are just like us, but is less well suited to the rest of the world. We will also become quick to complain but slow to offer help.

People who treat their Christian faith in this way miss out on the joy and privilege of serving others, and so becoming more like Jesus, who "came not to be served but to serve, and to give his life as a ransom for many" (Mark 10:45).

The church isn't just a community of Christians. It doesn't exist purely for the sake of the people who are in it. Instead, Jesus said that Christians are to stand out—to "shine" in a dark world:

 MATTHEW 5:14-16

¹⁴ You are the light of the world. A city set on a hill cannot be hidden. ¹⁵ Nor do people light a lamp and put it under a basket, but on a stand, and it gives light to all in the house. ¹⁶ In the same way, let your light shine before others, so that they may see your good works and give glory to your Father who is in heaven.

Is Jesus' view of the local church bigger than yours? How?

The picture Jesus uses is very vivid, and implies that Christians are a "light" that is clearly visible in, and makes a great impact on, the dark world around them. Ask the group how that compares with the way they see themselves and their local church.

You may want to remind the group of Vermon's illustration of this passage. He said this: "It is pitch black—you can't see your hand in front of your face. All around you are people who are lost and don't know where to go. Horrible things are lurking in the dark to trip them up and harm them. But your little *group are standing on a hill top. You are ablaze with light. All around you people turn to see a clear, bright light burning steadily without flickering. They start to walk toward you…"*

▶ **WATCH DVD 1.2** (9 min 42 sec) **OR DELIVER TALK 1.2** (see page 34)

* *Encourage the group to make notes as they watch the DVD or listen to the talk. There is space for notes on page 17 of the Handbook.*

Discuss

We are a unique people:
- **Born again**
- **Adopted into a new family**
- **We have moved from light to darkness**
- **A new creation**
- **Having eternal life**

The Bible uses these pictures, among others, to show how we become different when we respond to the gospel. Which of these descriptions excites you most? Why?

There isn't a "correct" answer to this question—it is designed to encourage group discussion.

The five examples given in the question can be found in the following Bible verses. You may want to look these up in advance to help you explain each concept (there will not be time during the group session).

- Born again: 1 Peter 1:23
- Adopted into a new family: Ephesians 1:5
- We have moved from light into darkness: 1 Peter 2:9
- A new creation: 2 Corinthians 5:17
- Having eternal life: John 5:24

In 1 Peter 2:9, Peter says that God has called us "out of darkness into his marvelous light." Why is it so important that we do not forget what we have been saved from (the "darkness")?

There are lots of potential answers to this question, so try not to let it take too long. You may want to steer the group to think of answers that tie in with the idea of Christians as light. If we are going to be "the light of the world," we need to remember what it is like to be living in darkness, and why the gospel is such good news for people who are in the dark. If we are going to "let [our] light shine before others," we need to remember that we were once just the same as them, and not look down on them.

▶ **WATCH DVD 1.3** (4 min 12 sec) **OR DELIVER TALK 1.3** (see page 34)

* *Encourage the group to make notes as they watch the DVD or listen to the talk. There is space for notes on page 18 of the Handbook.*

Discuss

When Christians talk about being different than the world, they often focus on the things they do not do—getting drunk, watching porn on TV, stealing stationery from work, etc. What is the downside of this approach to thinking about our distinctiveness as believers?

We can become very legalistic, just focusing on the things we need to avoid, and looking down on anyone who does them.

Living as a Christian may come across as just about rule-keeping and/or living a boring life—rather than our lives reflecting God's light: his goodness, beauty, joy, generosity…

The risk is that those around us may indeed see Christians as "different," but not find that difference attractive in any way.

How would you describe Christian distinctiveness positively, but not proudly?

There's more than one way you could answer this question:

- You could make a list of positive characteristics such as: Christians are generous, joyful, content, loving, willing to go out of their way for other people, merciful, forgiving…

- You could use an existing Bible list such as 1 Corinthians 13:4-7, Galatians 5:22-23 or Colossians 3:12-14.
- You could give a more general answer such as the fact that God is working in our lives through the Holy Spirit to make us more and more like his Son. Just as Jesus is pure and loving, so his followers are becoming purer and more loving. Just as Jesus came to be a servant, so his followers want to serve others. Just as Jesus faithfully obeyed his Father in all things, so Christians will want to live in the way we are shown in God's word, the Bible.

Pray

This curriculum looks at the qualities and character that should mark our lives as we grow as believers.

Pray that as you all work through this curriculum, you will understand more deeply who we have been made in Christ, and that you will reflect this as a church family.

Pray that you will grow in the qualities listed above and, as a result, shine more brightly in the world around you.

DAILY BIBLE DEVOTIONALS

As you finish the session, point group members to the daily devotionals to do at home over the course of the next week. There are six of them, beginning on page 21, and followed by a page for journaling. This week the devotionals walk through 1 Peter 2:9-10, where the apostle Paul reaches back into the Old Testament to give us a breathtaking view of what church is, and what church is for.

SERMONS

 OPTION ONE: MATTHEW 5:14-16

Vernon focuses on part of this passage in his DVD presentation, and you could expand upon it in a longer sermon.

 OPTION TWO: LUKE 5:27-32

This is the passage the Bible study is based on (see next page), which could also be expanded upon in a sermon.

 OPTION THREE: REVELATION 1:9-20

This passage is not mentioned in this material, but picks up on several of the themes of this session, especially the following:

- The Lord Jesus is the awesome, risen Ruler of everything.
- Each church—each lampstand—belongs to Jesus, and exists to shine forth the glory of his light.

If one of your Sunday sermons is to be based on the theme of this session, church members will find a page to write notes on the sermon on page 31 of their Handbooks.

BIBLE STUDY

AIM: The main teaching session this week encouraged us to think about how Christians are called to be a light *in* the darkness—and a light *for* the darkness. This Bible study shows how the Lord Jesus modeled this truth in his life and ministry, and will remind us that the gospel is where it all starts.

Discuss

Christians are called to be different. But we have often thought about our difference as being defined by the things we do *not* do. What are the advantages and disadvantages of this approach?

> People may talk about Christian attitudes toward alcohol, what kind of TV we watch, a particular approach to manners and a way of use of language, or other things. Christians should certainly be distinct in many of these areas—not given to swearing or drunkenness for example. But the disadvantage is that it quickly turns into legalism. I am a Christian if I don't do these things—and am not if I do. It also tends to be very selective. Gossip, gluttony and greed are thought little of, whereas a cigarette smoker can be unfairly demonized.

READ LUKE 5:27-32

> *31 And Jesus answered them, "Those who are well have no need of a physician, but those who are sick. 32 I have not come to call the righteous but sinners to repentance."*

Tax collectors were hated by the Jews, as they were regarded as collaborators with the occupying Roman forces.

1. **What is remarkable about what Jesus says and who he says it to?**
   - It is a very simple instruction: "Follow me" (v 27). The challenge to follow Jesus is at the heart of the gospel message.
   - It is made to someone who is effectively a traitor against the people of Israel.
   - It is a simple, clear and unequivocal command for him to obey, but it has huge implications for his life and lifestyle.

2. What is remarkable about Levi's response?

- He follows! And he leaves everything behind. It is complete, final and totally committed.
- He then throws a massive party for Jesus at his house, inviting many other tax collectors and assorted "sinners" both to celebrate with him and meet with Jesus.

What would it have cost Levi to follow Jesus?

- *Financial:* He would have been made wealthy by his work. He has lost his income, and presumably all the things associated with it.
- *Influence and power:* He would have had a position of power and influence over people, and with the Romans. All gone.
- *Personal dignity:* He immediately faces persecution from the authorities.

Additional question: What is the connection between following Jesus and faith in Jesus?

Following Jesus means that you trust Jesus to supply what you need. It shows that you are prepared to do as he says. It means that you are identifying with him and his other followers. It means that you are prepared to leave behind other things (repentance).

3. How do the Pharisees and teachers of the law respond (v 30)? What is behind their complaint, do you think?

They are scandalized that Jesus—a popular preacher who is calling people to trust and follow the God of Israel—would associate with such sinful people, and want to spend time and be seen with them. Perhaps they thought that Jesus, as a preacher of righteousness, should condemn those who were traitors to Israel. Perhaps they thought that these people were beneath them, and not able to be restored, rescued or saved. Their criticism reveals that they think of religion in terms of legalism—we get right with God by doing the right things.

This incident reveals that the Jewish religious authorities are:

- *Legalistic:* They think that they get right with God by being obedient to the detailed laws of God—not by God's forgiving grace.
- *Separatist:* They believe that they must completely separate themselves from sinful people if they are to remain "pure."

> *Elitist*: They adopt a superior attitude toward "sinners," believing them to be of less value than themselves.

4. **How does Jesus' response in verses 31-32 show them both who he is, and what he has come to do? How does his reply attack each of the three attitudes above?**
   - He is a doctor who has come to compassionately heal the spiritually sick. So it is quite natural and proper that he spends time with them.
   - Jesus requires repentance—gospel change—but does so in the context of a relationship with himself. The implication is that those who consider themselves righteous enough for God do not need him, and that he therefore cannot help them. Such an attitude is blind to the fact that we are all spiritually sick and need the medicine that only Dr. Jesus can give us. "While we were still sinners, Christ died for us" (Romans 5:8).
   - *Legalism:* Sin is a sickness that we need a doctor's help to cure—we cannot do it ourselves.
   - *Separatism:* This is not the correct response to the gospel—a saved sinner and a healed patient will want to bring others to the cure they have found.
   - *Elitism:* We can never feel this. We will always be "a sinner saved by grace." We are no better than even the "worst" sinner we can think of.

   To adopt any of these viewpoints shows we have just not understood the gospel properly.

5. **How can we as a church fall into the same trap as the Pharisees and teachers of the law?**
   - We can regard outsiders as enemies from whom we should keep ourselves pure. Church and our circle of friendships can become a "holy huddle" or a Christian bubble of niceness that disregards anyone outside itself. We end up being a club for ourselves, judging those outside as "unworthy" of being part of us, and effectively outside the possibility of forgiveness.
   - **NOTE:** Make sure that your group focuses on your own church—not on other churches. These discussions can too easily become finger-pointing exercises toward other churches—ironically, the very thing the Jewish leaders were guilty of—rather than a consideration of how we might need to repent.

6. **How does Levi illustrate what our own focus should be in the Christian life?**
   - He wants to publicly honor Jesus (Luke 5:29)—he throws a banquet for him.

- He wants others to meet Jesus, and discover the grace he has found in him.
- We are saved to serve, which we do by being mission minded—bringing people to meet Christ; bringing them under the sound of his gospel call to follow.

7. Who are the "tax collectors and sinners" around your church? How might we be guilty of treating them as the Pharisees treat people in this story?

It would be easy here to have a discussion about "extreme" cases—ex-offenders, pedophiles, vagrants, etc. Try to steer the conversation toward the more ordinary: rough teenagers, alcoholics, atheists, single parents, the elderly, those with low educational achievement, etc. Or even family members who seem to have no interest in the gospel.

How can we be more welcoming to them, like Jesus, and more open to encouraging them, like Levi?

The issue here is that often we do not even have casual contact with these types of people. We tend to be wrapped up in our own little Christian world, and not have time to socialize regularly with others that we might influence with our own lives and conversation. One aim that you might set for your Bible-study group during this study series would be consciously to start to build contact with people who are not Christians. We cannot let our light shine if no one can see it.

Apply

FOR YOURSELF: How are you living like Levi—in choosing to follow Jesus? When do you think you are most in danger of becoming a Pharisee in relation to your own holiness, and the sins of others? How will you help yourself and each other to avoid this?

FOR YOUR CHURCH: How "approachable" is your church to those who know they are sick and need a doctor? How might it feel like a club for holy people? How could it become more of a lifeboat for sinners?

Pray

FOR YOUR GROUP: Pray that you would grow as lights in the darkness as you work through this course together. Pray that the Lord would show you ways that you need to change and grow—and that he would give you the grace to do so.

FOR YOUR CHURCH: As your church embarks on this series examining what it means to be a shining light in the world, pray that you would grow together in seeing more clearly the light of the world—the Lord Jesus Christ—so that you will shine with his light in the darkness.

FURTHER READING

Lighthouses don't fire cannons to call attention to their shining—they just shine.
D.L. Moody

It is not scientific doubt, not atheism, not pantheism, not agnosticism, that in our day and in this land is likely to quench the light of the gospel. It is a proud, sensuous, selfish, luxurious, church-going, hollow-hearted prosperity.
Francis Chan

Some Christians never really thrive in holiness because they remain aloof and disengaged from other believers. But if we invest time and energy in making friends with Christians, we will begin to catch the lifestyle of light and replace the habits of darkness.
Richard Coekin

Books

- *Total Church (Steve Timmis & Tim Chester)*
- *The Gospel: How the Church Displays the Beauty of Christ (Ray Ortlund)*
- *You Can Really Grow, chapter six (John Hindley)*
- *I am a Church Member (Thom Rainer)*
- *Counter Culture (David Platt)*
- *Church Membership (Jonathan Leeman)*

Online

- *Who is the church? (video) gospelshapedchurch.org/resources311*
- *Have you been salty lately? gospelshapedchurch.org/resources312*
- *To engage the world means being present in it: gospelshapedchurch.org/resources313*

LEADER'S REFLECTIONS

SESSION 2:
A UNITED CHURCH
IN A DIVIDED WORLD

DIVISION, MISUNDERSTANDING AND SEPARATION SEEM INEVITABLE REALITIES IN THIS WORLD. SADLY, THEY ARE ALSO OFTEN REALITIES WITHIN OUR CHURCHES. YET GOD'S PEOPLE ARE CALLED TO BE DIFFERENT -- TO BE UNITED. HOW CAN WE ACHIEVE THIS WHEN OUR CHURCHES ARE COLLECTIONS OF SELFISH SINNERS?

TALK OUTLINE

2.1 Division, separation and segregation seem to come naturally to us. *Give examples from history or your local area.* Churches today can sadly reflect this tendency toward division—in who they aim to reach and in their ministry structures.

- The gospel brings people from "all nations" into a community. The church is described as being "one body"—it should be characterized by strong, vibrant unity.

2.2 **ONE BODY** *Ephesians 2:11-18*

- Ephesian society was full of division and conflict, along class, political, gender and racial lines—and especially between Jews and Gentiles.
- Broken **horizontal** relationships (with each other) come from a broken **vertical** relationship (with God). This is the biggest division in our world.
- Verse 13: Through the cross both Jew and non-Jew are reconciled to God—so we can be reconciled to one another as "**one new man.**"

ONE NEW MAN

- Christians are a **new race**—we all have the same blood flowing through our spiritual veins, the blood of Christ. Other identities allow for unique expressions of Christianity—but our primary identity is being "in Christ."
- Our churches need to be **multi-demographic**.
- This means we need intentionally to build relationships across barriers, be flexible about music styles, and train a wider spectrum of people for leadership.

2.3 **A POWERFUL WITNESS**

- A unified Christian community speaks powerfully to the world. *Share an example of Spirit-empowered reconciliation, such as the life of Louis Zamperini.*
- When something goes wrong with our body, we don't ignore it; we deal with it. The same should be true of our spiritual body when division and conflict happen.
- We were made for peace and unity, not division. When we let bitterness take root, we are no longer a bright, shining light, but a flickering, uncertain candle.
- The love and grace of Christ that reconciled us to God remains in us, so we can extend love and grace to others.

You can download a full transcript of these talks at
WWW.GOSPELSHAPEDCHURCH.ORG/LIVING/TALKS

A UNITED CHURCH IN A DIVIDED WORLD

* *Ask the group members to turn to Session 2 on page 33 of the Handbook.*

▶ WATCH DVD 2.1 (3 min 30 sec) OR DELIVER TALK 2.1 (see page 52)

* *Encourage the group to make notes as they watch the DVD or listen to the talk. There is space for notes on page 35 of the Handbook.*

Discuss

Vernon gave a number of examples of division, separation and segregation, both in history and that exist today. What barriers between people are common in your local area?

Use this question to highlight the main divisions and barriers in your own area. This will give you a context for the rest of this session. Depending on your area, possible answers might include ethnic mix, social background, age range, family units (single parents, cohabiting, etc), educational background… Ask your group to be as specific as possible, as this will help with later discussions.

👉 **EPHESIANS 2:11-18**

[11] Therefore remember that at one time you Gentiles in the flesh, called "the uncircumcision" by what is called the circumcision, which is made in the flesh by hands— [12] remember that you were at that time separated from Christ, alienated from the commonwealth of Israel and strangers to the covenants of promise, having no hope and without God in the world.

[13] But now in Christ Jesus you who once were far off have been brought near by the blood of Christ. [14] For he himself is our peace, who has made us both one and has broken down in his flesh the dividing wall of hostility [15] by abolishing the law of commandments expressed in ordinances, that he might create in himself one new man in place of the two, so making peace,

16 and might reconcile us both to God in one body through the cross, thereby killing the hostility.

17 And he came and preached peace to you who were far off and peace to those who were near. 18 For through him we both have access in one Spirit to the Father.

NOTE: Ephesians 2:11-18 is a complex passage with some tricky concepts in it. We are just going to focus on certain parts of it. For further help in unpacking this passage see *The Message of Ephesians* by John Stott (BST series, IVP) or *Ephesians For You* by Richard Coekin (The Good Book Company).

Before we became Christians, what was our relationship with God, and with others?

NOTE: Try to get the group to quickly see the big picture of how different Christians are now that we are "in Christ."

BEFORE WE BECAME CHRISTIANS

	Our relationship with God	Our relationship with others
v 12	• Separated from Christ. • Strangers to God's covenant promises. • Having no hope of a right relationship with God. • Without God.	• Gentiles (non-Jews) were alienated from Jews ("the commonwealth of Israel").
v 13	• Far off from God.	• Far off from others.
v 14-15	• People and God were divided by a wall of hostility.	• Gentiles and Jews were also divided by a wall of hostility.
v 17	• Far off from God; not at peace with him.	• Gentiles and Jews were far off from each other; not at peace with each other.
v 18	• No access to God the Father.	—

What happens to those relationships when we are "in Christ"?

WHEN WE ARE "IN CHRIST"

	Our relationship with God	Our relationship with others
v 13	• Brought near to God because of the death ("the blood") of Christ.	• Brought near to other Christians because of the death of Christ.
v 14	• No longer divided from God by a wall of hostility.	• All Christians, whether Jew or Gentile, have been made one in Christ. We are no longer divided from each other by a wall of hostility.
v 15	• Jesus abolished both the regulations of the ceremonial law and the condemnation of the moral law, to make us into "one new man," at peace with God.	• The ceremonial law was a huge barrier between Jew and Gentile, which Jesus put aside so that we can be at peace with each other.
v 16	• Reconciled to God through Jesus' death on the cross, so that there is no more hostility between us and God.	• All Christians are reconciled to God in the same way (through Christ), so there is no more hostility between us.
v 18	• Access to God the Father.	• We all have access to God in the same way, so this is no longer a barrier between us.

Additional question: Why is it so important for us to understand these changes?

This is who God has made us in Christ for all eternity. It is our real identity and our future. To live differently from who we truly are—united in Christ and called to live self sacrificially like Jesus—is to live without integrity.

▶ **WATCH DVD 2.2** (7 min 35 sec) **OR DELIVER TALK 2.2** (see page 52)

✱ *Encourage the group to make notes as they watch the DVD or listen to the talk. There is space for notes on page 37 of the Handbook.*

Discuss

Vermon said that "our broken *horizontal* relationships—with each other—ultimately come from a broken *vertical* relationship—with God." Can you think of some examples of this from your own situation?

"All people are in conflict with and separated from God—which is the root cause that leads people to living in conflict with and separation from one another." Ask the group if they can think of some examples of this in your own church or area, eg: a broken relationship with God leaves people looking for security or significance elsewhere, which then affects how they treat other people.

Ephesians 2 tells us that, through the cross, Christians have been made into "one body" (v 16). What do you think that means?

Without Christ, there was hostility between Jews and Gentiles. But when he died on the cross, Jesus created "one new man" (v 15)—a new humanity—out of the two. Followers of Christ, whether they have been Jews or non-Jews, now form "one body" (v 16). They are the body of Christ, the church.

How does this show why disunity matters?

If Jesus died to bring unity, then disunity isn't just "something that happens" and that we don't bother too much about. If we react like this, we are treating that aspect of the death of Christ as if it doesn't matter.

Ephesians 2 refers to Jews and Gentiles (non-Jews), but it applies much more widely than that. It tells us that the local church should be made up of the multiple ethnicities and/or social classes that are in the area. How does (or should) your church reflect your local area?

Apply these verses to your own church or group—to encourage yourselves where things are going well, and challenge yourselves where/if they're not. Use the answers to the opening question (see page 53) to keep this discussion specific to your church and area. Do the barriers you listed there mean that your church does not fully reflect the make-up of people living nearby? What does/should unity look like with people from different ethnic or social backgrounds? Or does your church include the same variety of people as your neighborhood?

▶ WATCH DVD 2.3 (4 min 42 sec) OR DELIVER TALK 2.3 (see page 52)

* *Encourage the group to make notes as they watch the DVD or listen to the talk. There is space for notes on page 38 of the Handbook.*

Discuss

What should we do when we are not united?

We shouldn't ignore it or assume that disunity is inevitable. Instead, like having a serious problem with a part of our body (or getting food stuck in your teeth!), we should work at putting it right as soon as we can. We should be "eager and diligent to do whatever can be done to promote reconciliation."

How can you put this into practice this week—as an individual, group or church?

Unity among Christians is so important that Christ died to make it possible, so this session may well have made some people uncomfortable as they consider conflict and division in their own lives. This is an opportunity to challenge people to do something about it—ideally this week.

If appropriate, encourage group members to be honest about any issues they need to deal with (while keeping confidentiality where that's important). Ask people to be specific about the areas they intend to address so that the rest of the group can be praying for them (and ask next time how they have got on).

Pray

"Unity among the different kinds of people within a local church is one of the most powerful witnesses we have of the truths of the gospel to our world."

Ask God to forgive you for any lack of unity in your church or group, or as individuals. Ask him to help you put into practice the things you listed above.

Pray that, as you do this, you and your church will be lights in a dark world, pointing to the reconciling work of God in your lives and the truth of the gospel message.

DAILY BIBLE DEVOTIONALS

Remind group members about the daily devotionals they can do at home over the course of the next week. This week the devotionals take you through Romans 12:9-21, focusing on some very practical ways that we are called to love those within the church, and those outside the church.

SERMONS

OPTION ONE: EPHESIANS 2:11-18

Vermon focuses on elements of this passage in his DVD presentation, and you could expand upon it in a longer sermon.

OPTION TWO: GENESIS 11:1-9; ACTS 2:1-13

These are the passages the Bible study is based on (see next page), which could also be expanded upon in a sermon.

OPTION THREE: 1 CORINTHIANS 12:12-31

This passage is not mentioned in this material, but provides us with a great image of the unity and inter-dependency of each church:
- We are all different, and so we are all needed by the body (v 14-20).
- We all need all the other parts of our body (v 21-24a).
- We are placed in our church body by God, to identify with each part of it and use our gifts to serve all of it (v 24b-31).

If one of your Sunday sermons is to be based on the theme of this session, church members will find a page to write notes on the sermon on page 51 of their Handbooks.

BIBLE STUDY

AIM: The main teaching session highlighted our unity in Christ—which needs to be matched with a unity in how we live as a Christian community. In this Bible study we will underline how this unity is part of the whole Bible story, and consider some implications for why we should work hard for unity as a local congregation.

Discuss

Why do you think there are so many different Christian denominations? What is good about this variety? What is less good about it?

Churches divide over all kinds of issues.
- Doctrinal: different understandings of certain doctrines, or a different weight given to certain doctrines over others
- Methodological: different approaches to worship and ministry methods
- Ethical: different approaches to key ethical issues—eg: alcohol
- Cultural: different styles of congregational character

Some of this might be very good. A church might need to fight for a certain ethical issue at a particular time; or defend a certain doctrine; or fight for the fundamental truths of the gospel when their denomination has abandoned it. And of course, it is important that a church is culturally approachable in order to win people for the gospel. We should celebrate variety as part of God's glorious plan for mankind.

But this kind of variety can also be negative. For example, when we use these differences to please ourselves, or to disown or denigrate others who think differently on certain non-core gospel issues. In general the world is mystified by the variety of Christian denominations, and believes it to be a sign that Christians are at each other's throats, that they cannot agree between themselves, and that there is no core truth in the Bible.

 READ GENESIS 11:1-9

⁶ And the Lᴏʀᴅ said, "Behold, they are one people, and they have all one

language, and this is only the beginning of what they will do. And nothing that they propose to do will now be impossible for them."

1. What unites the world that is pictured in verses 1-5?

- They have the same language and the same words (v 1).
- They are united in their pride—they want to "make a name" for themselves (v 4).
- They are united in their desire to have the same status as God ("Let us build ourselves a city and a tower with its top in the heavens").

In summary, they are united in rejecting God and pursuing a world that does not depend on him.

2. What lies behind why God confuses their language and scatters them? What would happen if they were not scattered?

- Their unity of language and purpose makes their desire for evil a powerful and dangerous thing: "Nothing that they propose to do will now be impossible for them" (v 6).
- Scattering and confusing them is actually a massive blessing to mankind, because when people are united for evil, they can do terrible things. It might be interesting to reference at this point how totalitarian regimes descend to the depths of evil, eg: Nazi Germany, Communist Russia and China, the brutality of North Korea and numerous other regimes throughout history and around the world today.
- Miraculously, this scattering also means that God's purpose for mankind to "fill the earth" (Genesis 1:28) has also been fulfilled.

Ever since Babel, we have lived in a disunited world. In the Old Testament, the 12 tribes of Israel—made up from very different characters (see Genesis 49)—were saved together and united to serve the true and living God. But even they could not stay united—they broke apart into two kingdoms (1 Kings 12). *How would God's purposes of unity be fulfilled?*

We pick up the story on the Day of Pentecost after the events of the first Easter...

 **READ ACTS 2:1-13**

⁵ Now there were dwelling in Jerusalem Jews, devout men from every nation under heaven. ⁶ And at this sound the multitude came together, and they were bewildered, because each one was hearing them speak in his own language.

3. Who was gathered in Jerusalem at this time (v 5-11)?

People from "every nation under heaven" (v 5). Get the group to see how diverse this group actually was: Jews and Gentile proselytes (converts) (v 11); Cretans (notoriously evil people—see Titus 1:12); and Arabians (descendants of Esau). Luke emphasizes that this is a wildly diverse group of people from every part of the known world.

What did the Holy Spirit immediately enable Jesus' disciples to do?

These first disciples—uneducated men of Galilee—miraculously spoke in the tongues of every nation that had gathered in Jerusalem.

What did they use this remarkable gift for (v 11, see also v 22-40)?

They spoke the good news about Jesus Christ—and called people to repent and believe in him.

4. What is the implication of this in light of what we read in Genesis 11?

- It is a sign that God's curse on mankind has been reversed in Christ. The language barrier has been overcome.
- The people who were scattered will now be united again as they respond to the gospel of Christ—but united in service of Jesus, not in opposition to God.
- The scattered nations who were seeking God will find God in the universal message about Jesus.

5. What are the implications of God's big plan for our view of the worldwide church (see also Acts 2:17-18)?

Jesus is for everyone. He will gather and unite the massive and wonderful variety of humanity into one people—and they will all share in the same Spirit and "prophesy" (= proclaim the good news about Jesus). The "universal" or "catholic" church (ie: all of God's people) is made up of people from every nation, race, tribe, social status, age and condition.

What are the implications of God's big plan for our view of "local" church (see also v 42-47)?

This unity and diversity must be displayed at a local level as well. When we fail to welcome, embrace and include the vast variety of human life, we are running counter to God's plan in the gospel for our life now and for all eternity. A miraculously united life together will be powerfully evangelistic in its effect (v 47).

What are the implications of God's big plan for our view of local and international disputes and division?

There may be ways to patch together unity among diverse people through education, policy and understanding. But the only way that deep divisions can be healed and restored is through the gospel. Our best contribution toward international peace is to preach Christ and see people come to faith in him.

6. Why is such unity in diversity so attractive to outsiders? Have you seen this working in your own experience?

It is unusual outside of the extended family to see such unity, love, concern and togetherness. Humans were made for such family intimacy, and when they see a genuine expression of it, they are naturally attracted to it. However, this kind of unity and oneness is remarkably rare. Some religious groups and cults are able to generate it by insisting that people lose their distinctiveness and become "clones." This is not true unity.

Sometimes our unity is shallow because our fellowship is shallow. We are able to maintain a theoretical unity because we do not intimately share our lives together. But when we are close to each other, the possibility for upset and disunity is much greater.

7. In your experience, what are some of the main obstacles to a genuine expression of warm, loving unity in the local church?

This could include many things—personal hostility (some people just do not "get on" together); clashes over styles of ministry and music; different doctrinal emphases; different ideas of how a church should be led, etc. Encourage the group to share stories of churches and situations where things have gone both badly and subtly wrong. It can also be the case that when you are close to people, small things can get unhelpfully magnified. Or we may have high expectations of other Christians who will inevitably fail us at some stage. What disagreements almost always comes down to is personal pride—insisting that my preferences take precedence over someone else's.

8. What do we need to remember when we face similar issues as a church?

- Unity is a work of the Holy Spirit in our lives. We need God's help both to understand and experience it.
- We need to keep reminding ourselves of the gospel, which tells us that we are all one in Christ Jesus. When we experience disunity, it should make us uncomfortable and uneasy—we must not feel free to leave it unaddressed.
- We must keep listening to "the apostles' teaching" and continue to share "the breaking of bread" (v 42), ie: reminding ourselves that we have so much more in common than that which may divide us.
- We need to keep confessing our sins to one another, ie: being open about our own failings so that we will not unhelpfully put each other on a pedestal.
- We need to keep submitting to each other in love—even over strong and heartfelt preferences for things like different music styles.
- We need to continue to rejoice and be thankful that God has called people from a rich diversity of life to worship and serve him.
- We need to keep extending forgiveness to one another for our failings—even when it's needed "seventy-seven times" (see Matthew 18:21-22).

Apply

FOR YOURSELF: Which particular part of being united with your fellow believers do you struggle most with? What cultural barriers do you most struggle to get over? What aspect of the gospel message will help deal with this?

FOR YOUR CHURCH: How apparent to an outside observer is the unity in diversity that you have in Christ? What might need to change so that you have more opportunity to both practice and showcase this unity?

Pray

FOR YOUR GROUP: Praise God together for the unity you have in Christ. Pray that you would remember the gospel that unites you, and work at the gritty realities of being united in your day-to-day experience.

FOR YOUR CHURCH: Ask the Lord to help your leaders when they are faced with particularly difficult or damaging disunity in the congregation. Pray that you would grow and develop ways to show your unity to a world that is hungry for it.

FURTHER READING

You are a Christian today only because God was the first to seek peace with you. You are now called and equipped to be the first to seek after peace and to attempt to pursue and maintain unity.
Thomas Brooks

Real unity does not come when we seek it directly. Rather, it is a by-product of seeking to follow Christ.
Tim Keller

We are not to be blind to our differences, but to appreciate our differences. If you are color blind, you miss out on the beauty of all that God has made. We need to rejoice in diversity.
Trillia Newbell

Books

- *United (Trillia Newbell)*
- *Blind Spots (Collin Hansen)*
- *Romans 8–16 For You, chapter eight (Tim Keller)*
- *Love (Phillip Ryken)*

Online

- *Why You Must Pursue Unity: gospelshapedchurch.org/resources321*
- *While the World Divides, the Church Kisses: gospelshapedchurch.org/resources322*
- *How to Weigh Doctrines for Christian Unity: gospelshapedchurch.org/resources323*
- *How Can Local Churches Work Toward Racial Harmony? gospelshapedchurch.org/resources324*

LEADER'S REFLECTIONS

SESSION 3:

A SERVING
CHURCH
IN A SELFISH WORLD

WE LIVE IN A "ME ME ME" WORLD. WE TEND TO SEE, AND WANT, AND TAKE. YET OUR LORD CAME NOT TO BE SERVED, BUT TO SERVE, EVEN AT THE COST OF HIS OWN LIFE. IN THIS SESSION, YOU WILL BE ENCOURAGED AND CHALLENGED TO TAKE AS YOUR MODEL THE KING WHO SERVES, RATHER THAN OUR SELFISH WORLD – TO LIVE WITH A "YOU YOU YOU" MENTALITY.

TALK OUTLINE

3.1 • • Watch toddlers play and you quickly see what's true for us all: **human beings are selfish**. We see, we want, we take. *Share a story from your own childhood.*

• Although adults may be more subtle, we are still motivated by a commitment to serving ourselves. *Share examples of how ingrained selfishness displays itself.*

• By God's grace, Christians must grow out of our old patterns of selfish behavior.

3.2 • **A SELF-SERVING WORLD** *Matthew 20:20-28*

• James and John imagine their place of privilege in Jesus' kingdom through a self-serving lens. But Jesus turns that perspective upside down (v 23).

• Verse 25: The world measures greatness as the ability to benefit yourself. "Did I get what I want?" If the answer is "yes," you have succeeded!

• *Share an example of advertising which appeals to our desire to have everything free and on demand, eg: flying first class with Virgin Airlines.*

• We even want "good things"—like volunteer work, our relationships with family, or sexual intimacy—to be according to our choice and convenience.

• The church of Jesus Christ is to be **radically different**—serving others at the cost of our immediate benefit and pleasure. This is what true greatness looks like.

3.3 • **A SELF-SACRIFICING LOVE**

• Verses 26-27: We are to be **slaves** of others. The Christian is to be someone who spends their life—their time, energy and resources—for the benefit of others.

• Verse 28: Jesus' example shows us that lasting greatness is found in **sacrifice**.

• Christian sacrifice will mean less comfort, time and money—and more inconvenience, tiredness, work, chaos and mess. Yet sometimes we even selfishly expect to enjoy every moment of our service!

• Serving is **investing**: our actions are reinvested by God into the lives of others.

• One day, we will stand before Christ to give an account of our lives. Will they be full and plump, because they were spent selfishly? Or will they look like his—with scars and wounds because they were full of cross-carrying sacrifice?

• **CONCLUSION:** We sacrifice out of the infinite storehouse of life that Jesus has given us. This *true* greatness will shine in the midst of a self-seeking world.

 You can download a full transcript of these talks at
WWW.GOSPELSHAPEDCHURCH.ORG/LIVING/TALKS

A SERVING CHURCH IN A SELFISH WORLD

* *Ask the group members to turn to Session 3 on page 53 of the Handbook.*

Discuss

You don't need to teach toddlers to be selfish—they naturally show the selfishness that is true of all of us. How have you seen that in small children, and in yourself?

This is a quick introductory question to start the group thinking about the issue of selfishness. Ask a few people to give examples from their own lives, or from children they know (eg: anyone involved in the children's work will have seen children try to grab the best crayons for themselves!).

▶ **WATCH DVD 3.1** (3 min 19 sec) **OR DELIVER TALK 3.1** (see page 70)

* *Encourage the group to make notes as they watch the DVD or listen to the talk. There is space for notes on page 55 of the Handbook.*

MATTHEW 20:20-28

[20] Then the mother of the sons of Zebedee came up to him with her sons, and kneeling before him she asked him for something. [21] And he said to her, "What do you want?" She said to him, "Say that these two sons of mine are to sit, one at your right hand and one at your left, in your kingdom." [22] Jesus answered, "You do not know what you are asking. Are you able to drink the cup that I am to drink?" They said to him, "We are able." [23] He said to them, "You will drink my cup, but to sit at my right hand and at my left is not mine to grant, but it is for those for whom it has been prepared by my Father."

[24] And when the ten heard it, they were indignant at the two brothers. [25] But Jesus called them to him and said, "You know that the rulers of the Gentiles lord it over them, and their great ones exercise authority over them. [26] It shall

*not be so among you. But whoever would be great among you must be your
servant, ²⁷ and whoever would be first among you must be your slave, ²⁸ even
as the Son of Man came not to be served but to serve, and to give his life as
a ransom for many."*

Discuss

**What do you think was the motivation behind the request of James and John,
the sons of Zebedee? Why might the other disciples have been so angry with
them?**

James and John want the place of greatest importance in the kingdom of
God, sitting at the right and left of Jesus. (In ancient kingdoms, this is where
the most important advisors to the king—those with the most honor and
authority—would sit.)

The other disciples were probably angry because they wanted the same thing.
(They had recently discussed who was "greatest" in God's kingdom—Matthew
18:1; Mark 9:33-34.)

NOTE: We're not discussing Matthew 20:22-23 in this session, but if anyone
asks about these verses, the "cup" that Jesus is referring to is the "cup of
suffering" that he will soon drink as he dies on the cross; see Matthew 26:39.

**What, by contrast, is Jesus' definition of "greatness" in the kingdom of God
(v 25-28)? Why would the disciples have found this hard to swallow?
Why do we?**

Jesus said that anyone who wanted to be "great" in the kingdom of God must
be a servant (v 26) and slave (v 27). This is the exact opposite to the power,
honor and authority the disciples expected and wanted. We struggle with the
same issues—our world thinks of leadership in terms of personal glory and
privilege, and we are infected with those notions of what true greatness involves.

How is Jesus a perfect example of self-sacrifice for us?

"The Son of Man [a title Jesus often used for himself] came not to be served
but to serve, and to give his life as a ransom for many" (v 28). Jesus is the Son

of God, and God's chosen King (the Messiah, or Christ), and yet he gave up his position of power and authority in heaven to come and live on earth as a human being. He came to serve us by dying in our place, giving his own life as a sacrifice for our sins. He is not merely our example (he is, supremely, our Savior) but he is never less than our greatest example.

▶ **WATCH DVD 3.2** (6 min 29 sec) **OR DELIVER TALK 3.2** (see page 70)

* *Encourage the group to make notes as they watch the DVD or listen to the talk. There is space for notes on page 57 of the Handbook.*

Discuss

"The church is to be radically and shockingly different to our culture in that they are a people willing to give up their whole lives for the good of others."

Share two or three very practical examples of how we can show this kind of sacrifice with our time, money or gifts. How will our natural selfishness prevent us from serving others in these ways?

Be ready to give an example of your own to start the discussion if necessary. Consider areas such as comfort, convenience, time, fame and power. This question focuses on how we, as individual people, can serve others—the following question considers the church as a whole.

"The church stands out within a self-serving world by being a community of self-sacrificing love." **How do you see this happening in your own church family? Are there areas that could be improved upon?**

Again, be ready to give a starting example if needed. Perhaps think about some of the ministry the church family is involved in and how that looks to those in the neighborhood. Make sure that you answer the second part of this question positively and practically, rather than being too self-critical or vague.

How does the gospel enable us to give our lives up for others?

Through Jesus, our greatest needs have already been met—forgiveness of sins, a right relationship with God and a certain hope of being with Christ in the new creation. In Christ, we know we are loved, approved of, and given all we need. This frees us from fighting for the security and significance that matter so much to those around us. Instead, we can use our time, money and gifts to serve others.

And as we appreciate more fully the gospel, we are changed to become more like Jesus, and moved to live more like him—the perfect example of self-sacrifice.

▶ **WATCH DVD 3.3** (7 min 20 sec) **OR DELIVER TALK 3.3** (see page 70)

* *Encourage the group to make notes as they watch the DVD or listen to the talk. There is space for notes on page 58 of the Handbook.*

Discuss

Sacrifice is hard! Why do we need to keep reminding ourselves that this is true?

Because we are naturally selfish, we want life to be easy and comfortable—to the extent that we may believe that if things are hard, something must be wrong. But giving up our time, energy and money is costly, so we shouldn't be surprised when things are hard. Instead, we should see this as normal.

"When we serve others sacrificially, what we give is reinvested by God into the lives of others." How have you seen this happen, as an individual or church?

The aim of this question is to help group members think of self-sacrifice in a positive way, rather than seeing it merely in terms of what we give up.

The Bible shows us that, even though God is all-powerful and lacking in nothing, he chooses to work through his people. This is a great privilege—and also a huge encouragement to keep serving him. Ask the group for some examples of this happening, where they have seen God take the things we give him and use them to work out his good purposes in the lives of others. Consider again some of the areas you've discussed earlier, such as comfort, convenience, time, fame and power.

Examples from the Bible might include the death of Stephen (Acts 7 – 8), which resulted in the scattering of the church and the spread of the gospel; and the sacrificial service and work of Paul and the other apostles.

Be careful not to imply that *every* time we serve God in some way, we will be able to see him clearly at work. Stephen did not know how his martyrdom would be used by God to further the gospel. You may know of godly missionaries who have sacrificially served on the mission field for many years without seeing a single convert. This does not mean that their service is pointless or unworthy in some way—we will not fully see how God has been at work until we are with him in the new creation.

What does selfishness look like in a church? How can you avoid this?

Try to imagine how your church comes across to those who live in the neighborhood. What is the biggest impression they will get of the church? Is it that you block up all the parking places on a Sunday morning? Or leave bags of litter on the street after a church event? Or play music too loudly during Friday-night youth group? Think about ways to avoid these kinds of problem so that your church comes across as loving and giving, rather than selfish.

And sometimes churches can be very loving and caring—but this is only ever seen by their own membership. The love and care is turned in on the congregation, and has no avenues of expression outside the fellowship. Get the group to look at the church program of activities to see how much is organized that is "outward looking." How could this outward-looking care be encouraged on a personal, individual level as well?

Pray

"Jesus, the leader of all leaders, the Son of God, the Lord of the universe, sets himself as an example of this for his followers: '... even as the Son of Man came not to be served but to serve' (Matthew 20:28)."

Spend some time praising Jesus for his immense self-sacrifice in coming to live as a man, so that he could die for our sins.

Ask God to help you become more like Jesus, so that your lives show the same love and self-sacrifice to those around you.

DAILY BIBLE DEVOTIONALS

This week's daily Bible devotionals study six Gospel passages which reveal to us how Jesus served people during his time on earth. They will thrill you as you see what Jesus has done and is doing for you—and help you see how you might serve others as a follower of the greatest Servant of all.

SERMONS

 ## OPTION ONE: MATTHEW 20:20-28

This is the passage Vermon looks at in his DVD presentation, which could be expanded upon in a sermon.

 ## OPTION TWO: PHILIPPIANS 2:1-30

This is the passage the Bible study is based on (see next page), which could also be expanded upon in a sermon.

 ## OPTION THREE: JOHN 13:1-17

This passage is not mentioned in this material, but it shows us how humble service was the core of Jesus' mission, and part of his call to his followers:

- Loving service: Jesus demonstrated his love in his humble service of his people.
- Gospel service: Christian service is most clearly seen in Christ's cleansing of his people at the cross.
- Our service: We are all called to live a life of Christ-like service, and to discover the blessing of living this way.

If one of your Sunday sermons is to be based on the theme of this session, church members will find a page to write notes on the sermon on page 71 of their Handbooks.

BIBLE STUDY

AIM: The main teaching session showed us how to be great in the kingdom of God—to be a servant of all. This is the pattern of the gospel—because Jesus, who was Lord of all, became a servant of all so that we might be saved. This Bible study on the whole of Philippians 2 reinforces this teaching, gives some practical examples of sacrificial service in action, and will encourage the group to get practical about their own attitude to serving others.

This study covers a lot of ground: a whole chapter of Philippians which has lots of detail and ideas in it. The aim is to give the group members a feel for the big ideas. So try to push the study along so that they get to spend time on detailed application.

Discuss

Who have been your greatest role models for the Christian life? What was it about them that you found attractive and challenging?

Allow the group to talk about Christians who have influenced them. Don't make any comments at this stage; just note the kinds of qualities that people mention, and then pick them up in the final question below.

READ PHILIPPIANS 2:1-30

¹ So if there is any encouragement in Christ, any comfort from love, any participation in the Spirit, any affection and sympathy, ² complete my joy by being of the same mind, having the same love, being in full accord and of one mind.

* *As people read the passage, encourage them to spot the four examples of self-sacrificial service in this chapter.*

In this famous passage we see how the good news of the gospel leads to people who are united in Christ and willing to follow his example of sacrificial service.

1. **What four things that come to us through the gospel does Paul point to in verse 1? How should each of these lead to the unity described in verse 2?**

77

Encourage the group to see how each of these things is a part of the good news we receive as believers. Get them to articulate how each one comes from the gospel message.

- *Encouragement in Christ.* By receiving Jesus we are encouraged, helped and called to live a life like his. When we are sacrificial servants, it means that our fellowship and community are no longer driven by selfish motives that drive people into factions or away from each other.
- *Comfort from love.* Knowing the love of God in the death of Christ for us, we can be confident that his love will never fail us, let us down, or let us go (see Romans 8:31-32). Division is often fueled by insecurity. If we are secure in the love of God for us, we will not strive to advance our reputation or win the love and approval of people—which so often come at the expense of others.
- *Participation in the Spirit.* All those who belong to Christ have received the gift of his Holy Spirit. The Holy Spirit gives us love for one another, and enables us to be God's people together. That's why, in the words of the prayer called "the grace," we say: "… and the fellowship of the Holy Spirit…" (see 2 Corinthians 13:14).
- *Affection and sympathy:* In Christ we no longer look only to our own needs. God pours his love for others into our hearts—especially love for other Christians—so that we care for them and feel the bond of family with them. We have familial love for other Christians, but we also look differently at others who are not believers (see 2 Corinthians 5:16).

2. How should Christians treat each other (verses 3 and 4)?

With kindness and generosity:
- Not being selfish
- Not putting themselves or their ambitions first

With humility:
- Not looking for glory or praise for themselves
- Considering others better than themselves
- Putting other people's needs or interests first

What stops us from doing this?

- Selfish ambition or vain conceit
- Thinking we are better than other people
- Putting our own interests first

3. **In verses 5-11 Jesus is revealed as God, as our Servant King, and as reigning in triumph. He chose to be born as a human being so that he could die on the cross in our place. How does this make you feel?**

Verses 5-11 are a wonderful summary of who Jesus is and what he did for us. Help the group to express some of the emotions that are natural when we understand the facts of the gospel and realize the amazing love and grace of Jesus toward us. Answers might include:
- We should feel humbled by his love for us.
- We should feel thankful to Jesus for what he did for us.
- We should be full of joy because Jesus has saved us.

4. **How do verses 6-8 show us what it means to have Christ's "mind"?**

Being a disciple means being a follower of Jesus. We should be growing like him in his love, humility, compassion, and willingness to be our servant. Jesus loved us so much that he was willing to suffer and die for us. The gospel teaches us that we are sinners for whom Christ died. This leaves us no room for pride in ourselves or in our own efforts. If we are following him, we must give up our pride and be willing to serve him and others in the same way.

5. **How does Jesus' humble, serving sacrifice for us transform the commands we are given in verses 12-18?**

We are *not* living like this in order to gain the presence of God, but because we have already been brought into the presence of God through Jesus serving us. It is our joy, privilege and calling to show to each other the grace that has been shown to us. We have been made holy through Christ. We are being urged to let that holiness shine through our actions.

NOTE: What does Paul mean when he says: "Work out your own salvation with fear and trembling" (v 12)? We need to keep working to make sure that we live like a person who has been saved by God. Make sure your group understands that this does not mean working *for* our salvation. Christ has already done all that is needed to save us. Once we are saved, our salvation will begin to work itself out in our lives in many ways.

You may find it helpful to use the house illustration: when you move to a new house, there is an actual moving-in day. But then there is plenty of ongoing work to get on with, as you change your house to become more and more like the home you want it to be.

We work out our salvation "with fear and trembling" because God is our Creator and Ruler. He is all-powerful and holy. Therefore we should be serious about how we relate to him. Proverbs 1:7 says that "the fear of the LORD is the beginning of knowledge." Of course, we also need to remember that God is our loving Father, who we can come to at any time with our needs.

Where does the strength come from to obey God's will in these ways?

It is hard not to grumble and be disputatious (Philippians 2:14). It is hard to live godly lives in a crooked and twisted generation. It is hard to shine as lights in the world (v 15). But living like this is the work of God in us (v 13). We need to depend on him to work this change in our lives as individuals and as a fellowship.

6. **Look at the examples of Paul (v 17-18); Timothy (v 19-22); and Epaphroditus (v 25-30). How do each of these men model for us what it means to sacrifice ourselves for others?**

It may be helpful to split your group into three to think more carefully about each of these examples.

Paul:
- brought the gospel to the Philippians at great cost to himself (see Acts 16:11-40).
- is in prison and contemplating his death as he writes to them.
- is rejoicing that he is being used to bless the Philippians through this experience.

Timothy:
- is genuinely concerned for the Philippians' welfare (v 20).
- is prepared to be different (v 21), even though others are self-centered.
- served Paul and is happy to go to Philippi (v 22).

Epaphroditus:
- is a messenger from the Philippians to Paul (v 25).

- is a fellow worker and soldier: a committed believer (v 25).
- has been "longing for" the Philippians—he is deeply connected with them (v 26).
- was deeply distressed that they were distressed (v 26).
- nearly died for the work of Christ (v 30).

Which of these qualities would you like to grow more deeply in yourself?

NOTE: What does Paul mean by "a drink offering upon the sacrificial offering" (v 17)? If your group members ask about the meaning of verse 17, explain that a drink offering was an Old Testament offering (a gift to God) of wine or water. Sometimes in the Old Testament, when animals were sacrificed, a drink offering was poured on top of the sacrifice. Paul is saying that the faith of these Christians and their work for the Lord is like an Old Testament sacrifice. Paul might have to die for the gospel. If this happens, it will be like a drink offering. His life will be given to God with the sacrifice (the faith and work) of the Philippian Christians.

This curriculum is called *Gospel Shaped Living*. This chapter shows how our new life and our lifestyle as believers are rooted in, inspired by and flow from the gospel of Christ crucified, who now reigns triumphant.

7. What are some practical steps suggested in this passage that we can take to grow more like Christ?

Encourage the group to read over the passage again and pick out the key points:
- Recognize that what we have is a gift from God in the gospel (v 1, 2).
- Remind ourselves of the love of Christ for us (v 5-11)—that is why the breaking of bread (Acts 2:42) is so important for a church fellowship. We remind ourselves that we are joined together through the death of Christ.
- Remind each other of our role now in the world. We are lights shining in the darkness.
- Work out the salvation we have received (Philippians 2:12) (see note on page 79).
- At the same time, depend on God to change us (v 13).
- We can learn from and be encouraged by the example of others.
- We need to hold fast to the word of life (v 16)—that is, keep focused on Jesus and the gospel. In practice, this is about reading our Bibles and being committed to sit under regular and good Bible teaching.

Apply

FOR YOURSELF: Which of the steps you listed in Question 7 do you most need to focus on at the moment? How can this Bible-study group help you to do that?

FOR YOUR CHURCH: How can you help each other not to be trapped by grumbling and disputation? How can you encourage each other to leave aside selfish ambition and conceit?

Pray

FOR YOUR GROUP: Spend some time praising the Lord Jesus for his amazing sacrifice for us. Pray that you would honor him by the way you live— following his mindset of love and care for others, and his willingness to serve us.

FOR YOUR CHURCH: Pray that you would love each other more deeply— as Jesus loved us. Pray that you would increasingly encourage each other to shine like stars in the world.

FURTHER READING

The Dead Sea is the dead sea because it continually receives and never gives.
Anonymous

You have not lived until you have done something for someone who can never repay you.
John Bunyan

The only way to get our service of Jesus right is to realize that supremely, we don't serve him. He serves us. First and foremost, Christians are not servants; they are served.
John Hindley

Books

- *Serving Without Sinking (John Hindley)*
- *Weakness is the Way (J.I. Packer)*
- *The Freedom of Self-Forgetfulness (Tim Keller)*
- *Total Church (Steve Timmis & Tim Chester)*
- *Blind Spots, chapter two (Collin Hansen)*

Online

- *Loving the Unlovely and Unwanted: gospelshapedchurch.org/resources331*
- *The Offence of Selfless Loves (video): gospelshapedchurch.org/resources332*
- *C.S. Lewis on Selfishness vs. Self-Interest: gospelshapedchurch.org/resources333*
- *The Ridiculous Grace of Adoption: gospelshapedchurch.org/resources334*
- *Loving Difficult People: gospelshapedchurch.org/resources335*

LEADER'S REFLECTIONS

SESSION 4:

A GENEROUS CHURCH

IN A STINGY WORLD

THE GREAT REFORMER MARTIN LUTHER ONCE SAID THAT
THE LAST PLACE A MAN IS CHANGED BY THE GOSPEL IS IN
HIS WALLET. FIVE HUNDRED YEARS LATER, THAT IS STILL
TRUE. OUR BANK STATEMENTS SHOW MUCH ABOUT HOW
DEEPLY WE HAVE GRASPED THE GOSPEL. WONDERFULLY,
WHAT WE DO WITH OUR MONEY CAN ALSO HAVE A
GREAT IMPACT FOR THE GOSPEL. SO HOW DOES, AND HOW
SHOULD, THE GOSPEL SHAPE YOUR FINANCES?

TALK OUTLINE

4.1 Statistics show that charitable giving is declining at the same time as personal wealth and spending are increasing. We are naturally tight-fisted—we hold on tightly to our money, time, possessions and privileges. Why?
- We like to consume for our own pleasure.
- We are afraid that we won't have enough for ourselves.
- When we do give, we want to be recognized, applauded and appreciated for it.

Christ's church should stand out as **an island of generosity in a sea of stinginess**.

4.2 **THE MACEDONIAN EXAMPLE** *2 Corinthians 8:1-7*
- The Macedonian church were **enormously generous, yet extremely poor**. They had to beg Paul to be allowed to give to the collection! How do we compare?
- The Macedonians weren't commended for how much they gave, but for **giving as much as they could**. Their model for giving is one of "**generous grace.**"

GENEROUS GRACE
- The Macedonian church gave in abundance. Generosity like this cannot and should not be compelled; it must come from an "abundance of joy" (v 2).
- We will be more generous the more we find our joy in God and his mercy; in our eternal reward secure in heaven; in knowing Jesus Christ. This joy stays abundant, no matter what we have materially.

GENEROUS *GRACE*
Grace is undeserved favor: Christ died for undeserving sinners. We should give to those who don't "deserve" it, without any expectation of getting anything in return.

4.3 **THE SOURCE OF GENEROUS GRACE** *2 Corinthians 8:9*
We were all **spiritual paupers** until God intervened. Christ embraced the poverty of the cross; through his sacrifice **great riches** come into our spiritual account. So generous grace is something we tap into from the already rich deposit in our lives. *Give examples of what generous grace would look like in practice in your context.*

CONCLUSION: We can answer a self-centered world with generous grace.

You can download a full transcript of these talks at
WWW.GOSPELSHAPEDCHURCH.ORG/LIVING/TALKS

A GENEROUS CHURCH IN A STINGY WORLD

Discuss

Imagine if we started this session by asking each person to tell the group how much they give to the church. Would you want to answer the question? Why / why not?

Try not to get bogged down with issues of exactly where people give their money, eg: whether it's just to church, or also to missionaries etc. as well. The idea is to start people thinking about how they would feel if other people knew exactly what they give. Possible answers might include: "It's private," "I'm embarrassed about how much I give," "I don't want to boast," "I don't want to be compared with other people," "Giving is meant to be secret" (Matthew 6:1-4).

▶ WATCH DVD 4.1 (4 min 3 sec) OR DELIVER TALK 4.1 (see page 90)

* *Encourage the group to make notes as they watch the DVD or listen to the talk. There is space for notes on page 75 of the Handbook.*

Discuss

"On average, Christians only give a little over $2 for every $100 they earn." Does this surprise you? Why / why not?

Inevitably, this statistic is quite general—it doesn't specify how wide a range of "Christians" it refers to—and it varies between countries. But even the statistics for conservative evangelicals show that our giving tends to be well below the 10% "tithe" figure that is often talked about. If you want to check out more specific figures, you could try the Barna Group (www.barna.org).

Again, don't get bogged down in a long discussion here—just register that this is both shocking (it's low), and not shocking (we are fundamentally selfish).

What are some of the excuses we give ourselves for not being more generous with our money and time?

These will vary according to the makeup of your group. They may include:
- "I don't earn enough to give any of it away."
- "I need to save for a rainy day."
- "I work hard, so I deserve a good holiday."
- "I don't want my children to have less than their friends."

What are some of the wrong motives we can have for giving?

- We want the praise of others.
- We want to feel good about ourselves.
- We think God will only be pleased with us if we give more.
- We give because we "ought" to give.

Optional follow-up question (if time): How can we as a fellowship sometimes encourage each other to have wrong motives or lack in our generosity?

- Help the group to see that this is a church-wide problem.
- We encourage each other in our selfishness whenever we affirm people in their choice to give to themselves rather than to others—often because we want to excuse the same instinct in ourselves.
- Wrong attitudes to giving are widely encouraged in the church: by offering recognition or public praise (donate this amount to the church-building fund and we will name it after you); by inducing guilt (if you don't give, then this missionary will starve); or by false promises (the Lord will bless you if you give).

▶ WATCH DVD 4.2 (7 min 36 sec) OR DELIVER TALK 4.2 (see page 90)

- *Encourage the group to make notes as they watch the DVD or listen to the talk. There is space for notes on page 76 of the Handbook.*

2 CORINTHIANS 8:1-7

¹ We want you to know, brothers, about the grace of God that has been given among the churches of Macedonia, ² for in a severe test of affliction, their abundance of joy and their extreme poverty have overflowed in a wealth of generosity on their part. ³ For they gave according to their means, as I can testify, and beyond their means, of their own accord, ⁴ begging us earnestly for the favor of taking part in the relief of the saints— ⁵ and this, not as we expected, but they gave themselves first to the Lord and then by the will of God to us. ⁶ Accordingly, we urged Titus that as he had started, so he should complete among you this act of grace. ⁷ But as you excel in everything—in faith, in speech, in knowledge, in all earnestness, and in our love for you—see that you excel in this act of grace also.

Discuss

How is "generous grace" a good description of the Macedonian church?

They were extremely poor (v 2), and yet they gave beyond their means (v 3). They were so desperate to give that they begged for permission (v 4).

Why are these two words inseparable as we think about this subject?

"Grace" means being treated in a way we don't deserve. It is being given something generously when we have no right to it. Understanding that we have received grace from God is the only thing that can motivate us to give in a truly generous way (ie: without regard to whether someone deserves the gift or not).

We often find it especially hard to give to people who we think are undeserving. How does the gospel help us with this?

As we saw in last week's session, Jesus is the prime example of self-sacrifice, and we are to be like him. We did not (and could not) do anything to "earn" forgiveness; we don't deserve it—it is a free gift through the death of Jesus. Because we have been shown such grace by Christ, we are to show the same grace to those around us, whether or not we think they deserve it.

▶ WATCH DVD 4.3 (5 min 41 sec) OR DELIVER TALK 4.3 (see page 90)

* *Encourage the group to make notes as they watch the DVD or listen to the talk. There is space for notes on page 78 of the Handbook.*

Discuss

Many churches have an annual Sunday when they focus on giving, after which we tend to ask ourselves: "How much *should* I give?" What difference would it make if we asked instead: "How much *can* I give?"

The problem with asking: "How much *should* I give?" is that it becomes a case of rule-keeping. We're not giving generously or joyfully, but merely because we "should." It also encourages people to set their giving at a particular level and then leave it at that for the rest of the year.

When we ask: "How much *can* I give?" we have the freedom to give generously (ie: more than an arbitrary set amount), but also to give in line with what we have. There may be times in someone's life when it is right for them to reduce their giving (eg: if they have been made redundant, or have a reduction in income for some reason).

What has God given you an abundance of (ie: more of than you need), which you can share with others?

This question needn't apply just to finances. For example, Vermon talked about a woman who has very little money, but who gives generously of her time and her prayers. It may be helpful for the group to suggest things that God has given other people—as they may not be aware of them, or be embarrassed to suggest them, eg: "John is terrific at listening—he always makes you feel that he has all the time in the world for you"; or "Angela is such a practical person—she just dives in and does what is necessary without being asked."

"We should stand out as an island of generosity in a sea of stinginess." **What will this look like for you as individuals? And as a church?**

Be ready to start the discussion about individuals with an example from your own life if needed.

When you talk about what this could look like as a church, there may be suggestions that you want to pass on to the leadership of the church. Think about the best way to do this and let the group know what you have planned.

What changes are you going to make as a result of this session?

You may want to give the group time to think about this individually and write down the changes they have decided to make privately. Make sure that the conversation does not just focus on individual financial giving—but on a wider range of issues with generosity. You might suggest that the first response should always be to mediate on the gospel—"they gave themselves first to the Lord" (v 5)—and only then to consider what their response might be. Some concrete actions might be: to pray about and review their giving; to encourage others in generosity; and to be more proactive in offering to help others. Try to make sure there's time for them to do this now—if they leave it until later, it's far more likely that they won't do it!

Pray

"Jesus lost everything so we could gain everything." **Spend some time praising Jesus for his generosity to you, although you did not deserve it.**

Ask God to help you become more like Jesus, so that you show generous grace to those around you.

Ask him to help your church to stand out as "an island of generosity."

DAILY BIBLE DEVOTIONALS

Do encourage your group members at the end of the main teaching session to keep studying, or start to study, the daily devotionals. This week they take a more detailed look at the passage that Vermon speaks from in his DVD presentation: 2 Corinthians 8 – 9.

SERMONS

 OPTION ONE: 2 CORINTHIANS 8:1-9

This is the main passage Vermon looks at in his DVD presentation, which could be expanded upon in a sermon.

 OPTION TWO: LUKE 19:1-10

This is the passage the Bible study is based on (see next page), which could also be expanded upon in a sermon.

 OPTION THREE: PROVERBS 19:17; 21:13; 30:7-9

These three proverbs are not mentioned elsewhere, but contain great wisdom for how to view our finances and prosperity (or poverty) as Christians:

- When we give to those who cannot give back, we are giving to the Lord, and we will find ourself repaid by him.
- If we are not prepared to listen to those who are financially needy, we cannot expect God to listen to us as those who are spiritually needy.
- There are spiritual dangers in experiencing poverty *and* prosperity—our prayer should be for neither, but simply for the provision of what we need.

If one of your Sunday sermons is to be based on the theme of this session, church members will find a page to write notes on the sermon on page 91 of their Handbooks.

BIBLE STUDY

AIM: The main teaching session this week has opened up the challenge for us to be people characterized by generous grace. We have been shown enormous generosity and grace by God in the gospel. When we are truly shaped by the gospel, we will display the same qualities in every area of our lives, both as individuals and as a fellowship.

Discuss

Think about someone you might describe as a "generous person" — what qualities do they have that earn them your respect?

Make sure that this discussion doesn't just focus on financial generosity. Often people will have a generous character which is shown by a gracious attitude to others in general. They will be people who are prepared to listen, talk with people and offer to help—whatever that might mean in terms of giving time, empathy or material support.

Where do you think their generosity comes from—is it their upbringing, their disposition, their circumstances or something else?

People can be disposed to generosity by all kinds of things such as: an experience of being helped out of poverty; gratitude at the circumstances God has put them in; or just the temperament they have—some women adopt a "motherly" attitude to everyone. Christians can and should be motivated by the gospel.

In this Bible study, we are going to look at a famous encounter with Jesus in Luke's Gospel.

READ LUKE 19:1-10

⁹ And Jesus said to him, "Today salvation has come to this house, since he also is a son of Abraham. ¹⁰ For the Son of Man came to seek and to save the lost."

1. What is the evidence in the passage that Zacchaeus was considered to be an outcast from the kingdom of God?

- Zacchaeus was a tax collector—and that involved collaboration with the Roman authorities. Not only that, but he was a "chief" tax collector, presumably having many others working under him (v 2).
- As a result Zacchaeus was hated and despised—he would have been viewed as a traitor (v 7).
- The suggestion of the wording in verse 9 is that Zacchaeus was not considered to be a "son of Abraham," ie: an heir to the promises of God to his people.

Why had he given up his reputation?

We're not told, but money seems the most likely candidate.

2. What does the way in which Zacchaeus seeks Jesus tell us about him?

- He does something undignified for a man in his position—he climbs a tree—which suggests an earnestness in his desire to see Jesus.
- When Jesus announced that he was coming to Zacchaeus' house, Zacchaeus "received him joyfully" (v 6).

3. How does this story show us the pattern of the gospel: God's grace toward undeserving sinners?

- Jesus initiates their relationship by commanding Zacchaeus to come down (v 5).
- Jesus calls Zacchaeus into intimate friendship with him.
- Zacchaeus does not deserve this. Whatever the fault with the assessment of the people, he is still a sinner. He has collaborated with the enemy of the state and has cheated people (v 8).

4. How does Zacchaeus' statement in verse 8 reveal the depth and reality of his response to the gospel invitation?

- He calls Jesus "Lord."
- He gives half his wealth to the poor. This demonstrates his response to the grace of God shown to him. He is prepared to bless those who are poor.
- He makes restoration to those he has cheated. This was similar in nature to the response demanded by the law (see Exodus 22:1).

What had changed him from a money grabber to a money giver?

He had found in Jesus what he was looking for in money: security, satisfaction and significance. It may be that he had begun to recognize that he wasn't getting these things from his wealth.

5. **What advice would you give to a new Christian who asked you about what they should do with their money?**

- It does not belong to them—it belongs to the Lord; and we are called to wisely steward our resources to bring glory to the owner: God.
- Under God we have many responsibilities to use our money wisely, including providing for our family, and being responsible for our future (eg: pensions).
- But we also have responsibilities to support the work of the gospel, our local church, and to provide for those who are in genuine need.
- We should not think about a tithe, but about being generous, ie: not: "How much *should* I give?" but: "How much *can* I give?"
- The size of our giving is less important than our heart (see Luke 21:1-4).
- We should not give in an ostentatious way, but quietly, secretly and humbly—not looking for approval from anyone but the Lord (Matthew 6:1-4).

6. **How will the love of money always remain a temptation for Christians? How can we prevent it from ensnaring us?**

- We must always beware of the power of money to enslave us.
- We must be aware that we will always make excuses for ourselves about why we should not give more.
- By and large, people are not very good at talking about money with each other. We must get over this hurdle and find ways of encouraging each other to be more generous.
- We are particularly vulnerable with regard to our children. It is possible to justify any expenditure for "their sake." But we need to think clearly about what we might be teaching them if we are prepared to spend lavishly on them.
- Plan a regular review of your planned giving to gospel work. Again, each year ask the question: "How much *can* I give?", not: "How much *should* I give?"

Apply

FOR YOURSELF: Where do you look for security, satisfaction and significance? How can you help yourself look to Jesus instead?

We look to finances, friendships and family, as well as our work, homes, and sometimes even our ministries as Christians. All these things can become idols that we serve. We need to remind ourselves that they will all ultimately fail us. We should be on guard against their subtle influence—and talk to each other about their failings.

Family in particular can become an idol for Christians. We can justify any expense for our children. Open up this subject and help people discuss how we can help each other combat our natural tendency to idolize our children.

The answer, ultimately, is that we need to keep being reminded of how big, permanent, and wonderful Jesus is compared with everything else.

Generosity will always involve money, but it is about so much more than money. What has God made you rich in that you can be more generous with?

Accept suggestions, but this might also be a good opportunity for group members to volunteer things they think others in the group are rich in. It may not be entirely obvious to the person concerned. Answers might include: prayerfulness; listening; practical support; empathy; wise advice; friendship; as well as practical skills.

FOR YOUR CHURCH: How can you as a church better express the generous grace God has shown to you in your congregational life?

As with the opening question, this will be about the character of our life and conversations, as much as it will be about programs for alleviating the needs of the poor. Some expressions of generous grace might be that:
- our conversations will involve a willingness not just to empathize with people's problems and to pray for and with them, but also to ask: "How can I help?"
- people will take the initiative to organize help for those in need—that may be organizing a food delivery or cleaning rota for someone who is ill, or offering help to individuals who are struggling with reading or applying for a job, for example.

- this willingness to meet people's needs at the cost of our own time and energy will naturally be offered to those who are visitors to our churches as much as to those who are members of the congregation.

Additional question: *"This story tells us that we have to give up our money in order to find salvation."* What would you say to someone who makes this claim?

It is not! Becoming a believer means putting Jesus first. We cannot do that if something else comes first in our affections. And money has a particular power to do that in us. "You cannot serve God and money" (Matthew 6:24). "The love of money is a root of all kinds of evil" (1 Timothy 6:10).

Jesus does not award salvation because Zacchaeus gave up his money (Luke 19:9-10). Jesus is making the point that his newfound generosity toward the poor, and his desire to make restitution to those he has cheated, show that he has experienced salvation.

On the positive side we would want to say that those who have found salvation in Christ will definitely have a new attitude toward generosity. The sign that we have received the generous grace of God in Christ is that we start to show that same generous grace to others.

Pray

FOR YOUR GROUP: Ask God to help you be discerning about the false motives that may take root in your heart. Ask God to fill you with a sense of his generosity to you in the gospel—so that you will be generous to others. Pray that you would find someone who is in need of your generosity—and that you would be prepared to give yourself to them.

FOR YOUR CHURCH: Pray that God would make you a grateful fellowship, and that you would abound in thanksgiving. Ask God to help your leaders know how to encourage generosity in the life of the church. Pray that any visitors would be impacted by the generous grace they see and receive from your church.

FURTHER READING

You can give without loving. But you cannot love without giving.
Amy Carmichael

Earn as much as you can. Save as much as you can. Invest as much as you can. Give as much as you can.
John Wesley

If our charities do not at all pinch or hamper us, I should say they are too small. There ought to be things we should like to do and cannot do because our charitable expenditures exclude them.
C.S. Lewis

Books

- *Sex and Money (Paul Tripp)*
- *Counterfeit Gods, chapter three (Tim Keller)*
- *Money Counts (Graham Beynon)*
- *Beyond Greed (Brian Rosner)*
- *Gospel Patrons (John Rinehart)*

Online

- The Time is Ripe for Radical Generosity: gospelshapedchurch.org/resources341
- How the Gospel Makes Us Generous and Content with our Money: gospelshapedchurch.org/resources342
- Generosity: The Key to Gospel-Driven Productivity: gospelshapedchurch.org/resources343
- Generosity (Theology Refresh: Podcast for Christian Leaders) (video): gospelshapedchurch.org/resources344
- The Gospel, Not Guilt, Motivates Radical Christian Giving: gospelshapedchurch.org/resources345

LEADER'S REFLECTIONS

SESSION 5:

A TRUTHFUL CHURCH
IN A CONFUSED WORLD

IN THE POSTMODERN WESTERN WORLD, TRUTH IS IN
SHORT SUPPLY — AND CONFIDENCE IN THE TRUTH IS
SCARCE, TOO. THIS SESSION CALLS US BACK TO A
ROBUST TRUST IN GOD'S TRUTH, REVEALED IN HIS SON,
ESPECIALLY IN AREAS WHERE TO LIVE BY HIS TRUTH IS
CONTROVERSIAL OR EVEN OFFENSIVE. BUT IT WILL ALSO
HELP US TO THINK THROUGH HOW WE COMMUNICATE
THAT TRUTH IN A WAY THAT HONORS HIS SON.

TALK OUTLINE

5.1 *What is the truth about life?* Many people are in a fog of uncertainty with no sense of absolute truths. Our own opinions and desires—and the voices of reason, science, etc.—are like quickly burning candles: providing some help, but dying out quickly. We need someone who can give the **true perspective**. Jesus...
- is **independent** of and **authoritative** over our world (John 1:3).
- overcomes sin and brings us out of darkness—he is the **light** that is full of grace and truth (v 14).
- *is* the **truth**—he embodies it (John 14:6). We can trust what he says to guide us. When making decisions about money, friendships, work etc., our vision is obscured by sin. But Jesus gives us clarity. We can shape our lives around his truth (8:12).

5.2 **TRUTH WARS**
Christians have found the truth in Jesus—but this will put us in conflict with a world that lives in darkness. The area of sexuality is currently an area of conflict:
- The world says that sex is something to pursue whatever the cost.
- In Jesus we discover that sex is beautiful and precious—designed for a man and woman to enjoy in the context of a committed covenant union.
- This perspective fits with the gospel story, which says that commitment, sacrificial service and love are the marks of humanity—that true love is more than a feeling.
God's people must be willing to **speak out** and **live out** truth in the way they love others. *Share examples of what this looks like in history and today.*

5.3 **SPEAKING TRUTH IN LOVE** *Ephesians 4:15-16, 25*
In Christ we're uniquely able to speak truth with love to the world. The church must:
- **"put away falsehood"**: increasingly live by the truth and line up with God's word.
- **speak truth** to one another: we are "members one of another" so the growth and health of the whole body is tied to the growth and health of each part.
- **love**: as we speak gospel truths, we need to live out the truths of the gospel in how we love—being kind, patient, gracious, humble, ready to serve, and so on.

Christ's truth puts us at odds with our culture—but the more the truth and love of Christ shine from our lives, the less attractive the world's "love" will seem (John 1:4).

You can download a full transcript of these talks at
WWW.GOSPELSHAPEDCHURCH.ORG/LIVING/TALKS

A TRUTHFUL CHURCH IN A CONFUSED WORLD

NOTE: We will be looking in detail at some of the Bible's teaching on sex and sexuality in the daily devotionals, so we are not focusing on that particular issue during the discussion time. But it would be worth being aware that these topics may be particularly difficult for some members of your group, so you may want to build in an opportunity for some pastoral support at another time if needed.

▶ WATCH DVD 5.1 (5 min 31 sec) OR DELIVER TALK 5.1 (see page 108)

● *Encourage the group to make notes as they watch the DVD or listen to the talk. There is space for notes on page 95 of the Handbook.*

Discuss

Can you think of an example from your own life of being in a fog of confusion that was changed by the truth of the gospel?

Be ready to give a personal example if the group struggle to think of anything. Possible areas where the truth of the gospel has brought clarity might include how we measure our worth or success, understanding why we are here, how to be a good spouse or parent, or what happens when we die.

What are some of the main areas where your culture diverges from Christian views and in which Christians find themselves increasingly in conflict? How has this changed over the years?

Answers will vary according to where you live. Recent conflicts between a Christian worldview and current Western culture have included gay "marriage," abortion and euthanasia. You may also ask: are there ways that the culture is actually *increasingly* reflecting Christian ethics/truth? It's easy to paint a picture of cultures being all bad, and increasingly bad; but there are times and ways in which cultures can become more like how God wants them to be, not less.

"Jesus doesn't just tell the truth—he is the truth." **What do you think this means?**

Everything about Jesus is true. He not only speaks truth, but he is:
- *"the true light"* (John 1:9).
- *"full of grace and truth"* (John 1:14).
- *"the way, and the truth, and the life"* (John 14:6).
- Jesus is the truth about God because he *is* God (John 14:9).
- Jesus is the truth about humanity because he is the perfect man.

Why it is wonderful that Jesus is full of *both* grace *and* truth?

Everything Jesus says is right and true, which means we can completely trust him. However, he also knows the truth about each one of us, and so he sees every way in which we have turned our backs on God. But because Jesus is full of grace, he doesn't condemn us. Instead, he gave his life as a ransom so that everyone who trusts him will be saved from their sin and brought into a right relationship with God (Mark 10:45).

▶ WATCH DVD 5.2 (4 min 49 sec) OR DELIVER TALK 5.2 (see page 108)

✦ *Encourage the group to make notes as they watch the DVD or listen to the talk. There is space for notes on page 96 of the Handbook.*

Discuss

"Jesus is full of grace and truth—what he says is right and loving." **How does knowing this help us answer the following accusations?**

- **Christianity is outdated**

Being loving and full of grace, as Jesus is, will never be out of date. Jesus is the Son of God, so he was not, and is not, limited to the time in history when he walked on earth as a man. The truth he taught then is still true now and always will be.

Christianity is intolerant

All of us are intolerant of some things (murder, for instance). God will not tolerate things that are evil, unloving or unjust—and we wouldn't want him to. And God is clear about how to live in his world—which lifestyles are obedient to him and are designed for humans to flourish, and which are not.

Christianity is judgmental

The fact that evil will be judged is good—nobody wants evil dictators or mass murderers to escape justice. In fact, it is reassuring to know that the person who will be their judge is the one person who has never sinned in any way (Acts 10:42). But that same person also makes it possible for us to be forgiven—no matter how severely others might judge us—if we put our trust in him. Further, everyone "judges"—because everyone says that some actions are right and some are wrong. A Christian seeks to align their judgments with the revealed will of the Creator, who knows what is best and who has the authority to say what is right and wrong. The difference is not that Christians judge and that no one else does, but that Christians judge according to God's word, rather than the view of their culture, family, etc.

Christianity is one view among many

Jesus doesn't allow us to believe this. For example, he says about himself: "I am the way, and the truth, and the life. No one comes to the Father except through me" (John 14:6).

Christianity is oppressive

We are actually oppressed by sin—it enslaves us, so that we cannot stop sinning. Jesus came to free us from this, since obedience to his commands is actually living in the way we are designed to, which will make us most satisfied (John 8:31-36). So oppression is life without Jesus in charge; freedom is found in obeying him.

"Truth is not a battle we win merely by making a better argument. It is a battle we win by living a better life." **What would this look like for you as an individual? And as a church?**

> What we say needs to be backed up by how we live. Ask the group for some examples of this, both as individuals and as a church family. Don't accept answers that are vague—encourage people to be really specific. In many ways our own life and our church need to model the truths in the previous questions—having a modern outlook where it does not compromise truth, being tolerant, not being judgmental, sticking to the one truth, and modeling the freedom we have in Christ. Be prepared to begin with an example of your own if needed.

▶ WATCH DVD 5.3 (6 min 17 sec) OR DELIVER TALK 5.3 (see page 108)

* *Encourage the group to make notes as they watch the DVD or listen to the talk. There is space for notes on page 98 of the Handbook.*

👉 EPHESIANS 4:15-16, 25

> **¹⁵ Rather, speaking the truth in love, we are to grow up in every way into him who is the head, into Christ, ¹⁶ from whom the whole body, joined and held together by every joint with which it is equipped, when each part is working properly, makes the body grow so that it builds itself up in love.**
>
> **²⁵ Therefore, having put away falsehood, let each one of you speak the truth with his neighbor, for we are members one of another.**

Discuss

What is the difference between "putting away falsehood" and "speaking the truth"?

> To "put away falsehood" will mean *removing* things from what we say—being careful not to lie, but also not to imply things that are untrue by what we say or how we act. To "speak the truth" will mean *adding* things to what we say—not just being careful to be truthful, but also willing to say things that we may find difficult or embarrassing, but which we know we should say in order to reflect the truth of the gospel.

What do you think it means to speak "the truth in love" (v 15)? When do we find this particularly hard to do? Or to hear?

"Speaking the truth in love" will shape both what we say and how we say it. We will be careful to speak truth, rather than lies, and to do so in order to build others up. We will think carefully and prayerfully about how and when we speak truth to someone, so that it helps them to grow in their knowledge and love of God, and to become more like Christ.

We can find this particularly hard to do when we are worried about how someone will react, or we're not sure if we are saying the right thing. (It may be helpful to discuss it with an older, wiser Christian first if we are unsure whether to speak to someone or what to say.)

We find it hard to hear when it means being shown our own sinfulness and/or we are being challenged to give up ungodly ways of living.

What goes wrong when we (as individuals and as churches) speak the truth lovelessly? Or when we seek to love others but without speaking truth? Can you think of examples from your own experience of these two equal and opposite errors? Which do you tend toward personally?

When we speak the truth lovelessly, we may cause unnecessary hurt or difficulty, and that will make it harder for the person concerned to accept that what we have said is right and true. They may reject what we say, and also the gospel message.

When we seek to love others but without speaking truth, we're not truly loving them. For example, if our church is good at providing things like night shelters and food banks, but doesn't also share the true gospel message with our neighborhood, we are not loving people because we are not warning them about the consequences of living and dying without Jesus. If we allow someone to live sinfully and unrepentantly because it makes them happy, we are not loving them, because their eternal happiness matters more than the fleeting happiness they gain from that sin.

Pray

"The light shines in the darkness, and the darkness has not overcome it" (John 1:5). Spend some time praising Jesus for being the true light.

Thank God for bringing you to know him through the light of the gospel.

Ask him to help you put into practice the things you discussed in this session.

DAILY BIBLE DEVOTIONALS

Vermon mentions in his presentation that the area of sexual ethics is one in which Christian truth and Western culture's views are in opposition. So in these devotionals, we will take a close look at Paul's teaching on love, obedience, sex and relationships in 1 Thessalonians 4:1-12.

SERMONS

OPTION ONE: EPHESIANS 4:15-16

This is one of the passages Vermon uses in his DVD presentation, which could be expanded upon in a sermon.

OPTION TWO: 1 THESSALONIANS 2:1-12

The Bible study is based on the second half of this passage (see next page), and it could be expanded upon in a sermon.

OPTION THREE: JOHN 4:1-30

This passage is not mentioned in this material, but shows how the Lord Jesus' truth offered both clarity and freedom to those he met:
- Jesus offers true life (v 7-15).
- Jesus knows the truth about us (v 16-19).
- Jesus is God's Messiah, through whom we are able truly to worship God (v 20-30).

If one of your Sunday sermons is to be based on the theme of this session, church members will find a page to write notes on the sermon on page 111 of their Handbooks.

BIBLE STUDY

AIM: The main teaching session this week has challenged us to speak the truth of God's word in a hostile world. This may take many forms, but must always lead back to Jesus—who is the truth. This Bible study tries to open up the reality of some of the hostility we will face in this, and to encourage us to model the love and grace of Christ as we maintain a faithful witness.

Discuss

Have you ever had to break some bad news to someone, or tell them something that will be hard for them to hear? What fears did you have beforehand, and what was their reaction?

> This might be giving someone a difficult appraisal at work, or having to fire someone; or it might be something at home—telling children about the death of a family member perhaps; or breaking up with a girlfriend or boyfriend. Try to draw out the feelings of fear about how people will react, a desire to soften the way you speak, the inevitability of having to say it, etc. There are a range of possible reactions to bad news: some people react with anger, or with tears, or with disbelief.

In this Bible study, we are going to look at how Paul viewed his approach to telling the truth to others. Paul is writing to the Christians in Thessalonica, whose church was born in troubled circumstances...

☛ READ 1 THESSALONIANS 2:1-12

> *¹ For you yourselves know, brothers, that our coming to you was not in vain. ² But though we had already suffered and been shamefully treated at Philippi, as you know, we had boldness in our God to declare to you the gospel of God in the midst of much conflict.*

1. What kind of reception had Paul been getting as he traveled around talking about the gospel? (See also Acts 17:1-15.)

- Hostility: The opponents of the gospel were jealous and angry.
- Persecution: Paul had been beaten and imprisoned in Philippi, and now in Thessalonica a riot had started.
- False accusations: Paul's message and reputation was dragged through the mud—caricatured. The gospel was mocked and used as a way of getting the apostles into trouble.
- But he was also welcomed elsewhere (Berea) and his words were embraced with respect and seriousness.

But what is his assessment of his mission? What is his reasoning for this?

He thinks it is a success:
- People had heard the truth about Christ (1 Thessalonians 2:2).
- People had responded to Paul's appeal to follow Christ as King.
- Paul and his colleagues were on a mission from God—the gospel had been entrusted to them, and they had faithfully delivered it (v 4).
- More than that, they had delivered it in an honest and straightforward way (v 3-5).
- God was pleased with them for their faithfulness.

2. What temptations are Paul and his friends clearly aware of as they travel around teaching others the truth about Christ?

- v 2: "We had boldness in our God to declare to you the gospel of God in the midst of much conflict." It was clearly a temptation to not speak. They needed to be brave and resolute in their mission, knowing that their words would provoke hostility.
- v 3: They might have been tempted to be manipulative—tricking people in their arguments to "get results."
- v 3: Their motives might have become tainted by pride, greed or spite, rather than to honor God.
- v 5: They might have fitted in with the pattern of other traveling teachers and demanded money, or else "played a part" to get people to like them and respond with flattery and false praise.
- v 9: They might have been tempted to stand on their status as God's messengers, and have demanded to be looked after—instead they worked very hard not to be a burden to those they were sharing the good news with.

3. **Gospel truth is a message that is conveyed by words. But what else is involved that enables the message to be clearly heard (v 6-9)?**

Words of truth must be shared with lives of love. Paul and his friends modeled the grace of God in the gospel in the way in which they behaved among the Thessalonians: being loving, caring, hard-working, and eager not to put any burden on others, so that the message would be adorned. They showed a determination not to let anything in their lives get in the way of people hearing the message.

4. **What are some of the "acceptable" messages we have for the world that flow from the gospel?**

There are many very positive things that most people would accept today:
- The love of God for us
- The dignity and worth of people
- Being part of a caring and diverse local community
- Care and generosity for the poor and needy

And what are some of the messages that might provoke hostility and debate?

There are many things that people will perceive as archaic, outdated and offensive in the gospel message:
- The reality of hell
- The need for a sacrifice to save us
- The reality of sin in our lives
- The Bible's view on gender and sexual ethics
- The exclusivity of Jesus' truth claims. In John 14:6 Jesus said: "I am the way, and the truth, and the life. No one comes to the Father except through me." Many people would be happy with the first part of the verse (although would not quite know what it meant); but they would be very offended by, and reject, the second half.

5. **So what might our temptation be as the opportunity arises for us to speak truth into our confused world?**

The same as the temptation for Paul and his companions:
- We might be fearful of any hostile reaction and keep quiet.
- We may be tempted to water down or adapt the truth to make it more palatable.

- We might be tempted to have false motives for speaking—ones other than love and compassion for sheep without a shepherd. For example, some Christians can be tempted to be aggressive, dismissive or derogatory against people who advocate gay rights, or who hold different political opinions.
- We can be tempted to "win an argument" by manipulative words; or ingratiate ourselves by flattery, so that people will like us.
- We can be tempted to be lazy.
- We can be tempted to be arrogant with the truth.

How can we encourage ourselves to remain faithful and focused?

- We need to remind ourselves that it is God's gospel of truth—so it is not ours to change (v 4).
- We must resist the temptation toward pride in the truth: "We know it: you don't." We only know the truth because God has given it to us.
- We need to remind ourselves and each other that we are seeking God's approval, not that of other people (v 6).
- We need to rest on God's strength (v 2).
- We must remember that sharing gospel truth with others is pleasing to God. He loves it when we share the good news.

6. **How important is it, do you think, to challenge public thinking about ethical and other issues in our society? What should we be focusing on?**

We should not shrink from declaring God's loving plan for life. But we also need to remember that *the gospel is the priority*. People will not really understand why we are so heartfelt about certain issues unless they have understood how it fits into a Christian worldview. At one level, convincing people that abortion or human trafficking is wrong, for example, will not get them nearer to God or eternal life—even though it may save a baby or free someone who is oppressed. So lovingly pointing others to Jesus, who is the truth, must remain our number one priority at all times.

Christians should also be strongly arguing for a wide range of issues in the public space, not just the headline ethical issues. We need to pick up the issue of the moment, but not at the expense of other, often larger issues which rumble along under the surface—child poverty, equal justice for all, or the need for scrupulous honesty and transparency in public life and in business, for example. All truth is God's truth.

119

Why is it important to keep verse 8 so clearly in our minds when speaking with others?

- *Our motive in truth-sharing should be love for others.* The truths we share may be hard, challenging, bewildering or outrageous to them, but this is the only truth that will truly set them free. It is therefore loving to speak it into their lives.
- *Our aim for truth-sharing should be to share the gospel with them.* The central truths about Jesus are the most important thing, so—over the course of a conversation or relationship—these are the truths we are aiming to get to.
- *We should not tell the truth to others without sharing our lives with them.* Sometimes Christians can engage in a conversation with the world that is like throwing grenades over a wall. We state truths, but quickly retreat into our own little Christian bunker. This verse makes it clear that true conversation is more than words. And if we truly love them, our truth-telling will be properly relational and pastoral in its character.

Apply

Pick one or two of the subjects below about which Christians will have something clear to say. Imagine that you are with friends for coffee, or standing by the water cooler at work, and the subject comes up. Work out how you might:

(1) express clearly and lovingly what Christians believe on this subject and why.
(2) humbly ask some questions of them that get deeper into the issue.
(3) make a clear distinction between what the Bible says for definite; and what it does not say, and what is therefore an area for discussion.
(4) simply show that this is part of a much bigger worldview which has a loving and just God at its center.
(5) take the conversation to Jesus.

Topics to consider:

- **Adultery**
- **Alcohol**
- **Lying and gossip**
- **The prominent failure of a Christian leader**
- **Abortion**

- Homosexuality and gay marriage
- What is the most important political priority for our government?

This exercise is not just about learning arguments to use against others. It should be working out the principles we have seen in this passage into a constructive attitude when engaging with others: "Speaking the truth in love." And context is all-important here. A conversation on abortion, for example, might come in different forms:

- A new abortion clinic that has opened locally, where someone (not a Christian) says it is a good thing.
- A girl from a Christian family who had an abortion, and has been thrown out of the home as a result.

In both, you will want to talk about the preciousness of life; the Christian instinct to care for and protect the weak, vulnerable and voiceless; and the heartlessness of a society that chooses this brutal act over nurturing life. But for the latter there needs also to be a discussion about how Christians can fail to be forgiving and can act hypocritically. As leader, watch out for the temptation to go beyond what the Bible says on some of these issues.

Pray

FOR YOURSELF: Ask God to help you know the truth more clearly, and be able to speak about it humbly and faithfully. Pray that you would help others to think clearly about how to communicate gospel truths in a loving and compassionate way.

FOR YOUR CHURCH: Pray that your church would be obedient to Jesus' commands to not judge others, gossip, lie or be insulting. Pray that you would be a church marked by loving truthfulness and clarity.

FURTHER READING

A dog barks when his master is attacked. I would be a coward if I saw that God's truth is attacked and yet would remain silent.
John Calvin

The early church was strikingly different from the culture around it … A pagan gave nobody their money and practically gave everybody their body. And the Christians came along and gave practically nobody their body and they gave practically everybody their money.
Tim Keller

The human heart longs for constancy. In forfeiting the sanctity of sex by casual, nondiscriminatory "making out" and "sleeping around," we forfeit something we cannot well do without. By trying to grab fulfillment everywhere, we find it nowhere.
Elisabeth Elliot

Books

- *The Intolerance of Tolerance (D.A. Carson)*
- *Meltdown (Marcus Honeysett)*
- *God in the Wasteland (David Wells)*
- *Counterfeit Gods, chapter two (Tim Keller)*
- *Is God Anti-Gay? (Sam Allberry)*
- *Sex and Money (Paul Tripp)*
- *The Stories we Tell (Mike Cosper)*

Online

- *Absolute Truth in an Upside Down World: gospelshapedchurch.org/resources351*
- *Holding Fast to Truth in a Doubting Age: gospelshapedchurch.org/resources352*
- *Speaking the Truth in Love: gospelshapedchurch.org/resources353*
- *Intolerable Tolerance: gospelshapedchurch.org/resources354*

LEADER'S REFLECTIONS

SESSION 6:

A JOYFUL CHURCH

IN A SUFFERING WORLD

WE LEARN MORE ABOUT OURSELVES AND ABOUT OUR
FAITH IN OUR SAVIOR IN PERIODS OF SUFFERING THAN
AT ANY OTHER TIME IN OUR LIVES. AND SINCE WE LIVE
IN A BROKEN WORLD, TO LIVE WITH JOY IN HARDSHIPS
IS A GREAT WITNESS TO THOSE AROUND US. BUT THIS
IS EASIER TO SAY THAN TO DO. HOW CAN WE TRULY
LIVE WITH HEARTFELT JOY WHEN LIFE IS FALLING
APART? AND HOW CAN WE HELP OTHERS IN OUR
CHURCHES TO DO THIS?

TALK OUTLINE

6.1 ● THE PAIN OF SUFFERING

- Losing your job or home; financial problems; illness; divorce. It doesn't matter how rich, pretty, strong or smart you are: no one can escape suffering.
- People react to suffering in different ways: anxiety, despair, anger, cynicism, renewed religious effort. But the Bible reveals a new way to look at suffering—a way to "lean into" it, grow through it, and have joy in the midst of it.

6.2 ● JOY EVEN IN SUFFERING *Habakkuk 3:17-19*

Habakkuk predicts a terrible scenario for a farming community (v 17), yet he responds with joy (v 18). How? He rejoices "in the LORD"—redirecting attention from his circumstances to his relationship with God. In suffering we must remember:

(1) God gives strength and stability (v 19). The mountain of difficulty may look insurmountable, but God will help us navigate it. His people will not fall.

(2) God gives saving hope (v 18). The suffering we face now *will* eventually end. This doesn't give us all the answers; but God has already done the *big thing* for our salvation in letting his Son die for us—so suffering cannot separate us from his love and will not destroy us. God has built the road to eternal joy at the cross; we must fix our eyes on Jesus for endurance and joy (Hebrews 12:1-2).

6.3 ● PRACTICAL WAYS TO EXPERIENCE JOY IN SUFFERING

- **Reject sub-standard Christianity.** True joy cannot be found apart from an authentic, substantial and active relationship with God through Jesus. Superficial "Sunday only" Christianity, prosperity-gospel Christianity, and legalistic Christianity don't work—they will fail to give us joy in suffering.
- **Invest in a healthy local church community.** Habakkuk 3:19 assumes that what is written was talked and sung about by the local congregation *together*. The church is the body of Christ—as we serve, encourage, forgive and love each other, we experience the service, encouragement and love of Jesus toward us.

● **CONCLUSION:** This joy is a powerful witness to a lonely, lost world. In the face of suffering, all the world can offer is sad clichés, but Christians have something substantial to offer: a Savior. We can say with Habakkuk: "I will rejoice in the LORD."

You can download a full transcript of these talks at
WWW.GOSPELSHAPEDCHURCH.ORG/LIVING/TALKS

A JOYFUL CHURCH IN A SUFFERING WORLD

NOTE: In this session we will be looking at the issue of suffering. This is an important topic since being joyful in suffering is one way in which Christians can shine particularly brightly among non-believers. However, it may be a current and difficult issue for some in your group. It would be good to think in advance about how you (or someone from your church family) can offer support to anyone who is suffering deeply, and who needs more help than is possible (or appropriate) during the group session.

▶ WATCH DVD 6.1 (3 min 29 sec) OR DELIVER TALK 6.1 (see page 128)

* *Encourage the group to make notes as they watch the DVD or listen to the talk. There is space for notes on page 115 of the Handbook.*

Discuss

Do you recognize the descriptions of the way people react to different kinds of suffering? How have you seen these in yourself and others?

These are the examples given in the DVD/talk. Be ready to suggest a few of them yourself to start the conversation, but don't feel the need to discuss the full list.

- We become anxious, worried or stressed.
- We despair or become depressed.
- We get angry with God.
- We become cynical or indifferent.
- We think we've done something "bad" to deserve our suffering.
- We strive to have more faith and/or give more money so that we "get the blessing" of health and wealth that we have been promised.

Have you ever known someone who has "suffered well"? What impressed you about them?

If group members are struggling to think of any examples of this, it may help to rephrase the question as: "Can you think of anyone who responded to their suffering in a way that pointed others to God's goodness and showed their trust in his promises?"

▶ WATCH DVD 6.2 (9 min 34 sec) OR DELIVER TALK 6.2 (see page 128)

* *Encourage the group to make notes as they watch the DVD or listen to the talk. There is space for notes on page 116 of the Handbook.*

☛ READ HABAKKUK 3:17-19

17 Though the fig tree should not blossom,
      nor fruit be on the vines,
the produce of the olive fail
      and the fields yield no food,
the flock be cut off from the fold
      and there be no herd in the stalls,
18 yet I will rejoice in the LORD;
      I will take joy in the God of my salvation.
19 God, the Lord, is my strength;
      he makes my feet like the deer's;
      he makes me tread on my high places.

   To the choirmaster: with stringed instruments.

Discuss

The circumstances that Habakkuk faces have not changed and yet he says that he is rejoicing. Why (v 18)?

Habakkuk speaks about having joy *even* in the midst of suffering. This is possible because he is focusing on God rather than on his circumstances.

What does Habakkuk know about God that makes it possible for him to rejoice (v 18-19)?

* He is the Lord (v 18, 19).
* He is the God who has brought salvation (v 18).

- He gives Habakkuk the strength and stability to face the mountain of suffering (v 19).

What do you think it means to have joy in suffering?

To have "joy in suffering" doesn't mean to be smiling all the time, or pretending that everything is fine. It's not that we treat the suffering as if it doesn't exist or doesn't hurt.

Instead, our source of joy is God himself—the relationship we have with him now, and look forward to in the new creation.
- If we are Christians, we know that no suffering, no matter how severe, can separate us from God's love (Romans 8:38-39).
- We know that God is good, and that everything he brings into our lives is used by him to help us to grow more like Christ (Romans 8:28).
- We know that Christ is with us in everything we suffer, and that one day we will see him face to face (Philippians 1:21).
- We can look forward to being in the new creation, where "the dwelling place of God is with man. He will dwell with them, and they will be his people, and God himself will be with them as their God. He will wipe away every tear from their eyes, and death shall be no more, neither shall there be mourning, nor crying, nor pain anymore, for the former things have passed away" (Revelation 21:3-4).

▶ **WATCH DVD 6.3** (4 min 33 sec) **OR DELIVER TALK 6.3** (see page 128)

* *Encourage the group to make notes as they watch the DVD or listen to the talk. There is space for notes on page 118 of the Handbook.*

Discuss

How could you answer the following in a way that points to both God's goodness and sovereignty?

- **"If you are suffering, you should pray to God and he will heal you."**

The Bible says that God uses suffering to work in our lives and make us more like Christ. In fact, he intentionally brings suffering into our lives for this reason. So we can certainly pray about our suffering, but he may not heal us, since he is the one who knows what will be best for each one of us.

● **"If God doesn't heal you, it's because you don't trust him enough."**

God is sovereign and is not limited by the level of our faith. If God doesn't heal us, it is because he knows that the illness is the best way to make us like Christ. This statement is cruel, wrong and extremely hurtful to those who are struggling with suffering. Certainly suffering is a time when we should examine ourselves, but we should urge people to trust God whatever happens.

● **"When life is hard, all you can do is grit your teeth and try to get through it."**

We would find life very hard indeed if this was true. This stoic approach to life is very common, but it is also very unspiritual! When we suffer as believers, we have the joy of walking through pain and suffering with a Savior who knows our frailty and understands what it means to suffer. And we know that God will give us the strength we need to face suffering (Habakkuk 3:19).

● **"If God loves me, why did I lose my job?"**

We must not judge God's love by our circumstances—and we don't need to! We know that God loves us because he sent Jesus to die for us. "In this the love of God was made manifest among us, that God sent his only Son into the world, so that we might live through him" (1 John 4:9). We may never know the precise reasons why certain things happen—they are often inexplicable. But we do need to encourage others to trust the Lord's love for his people when bad things happen.

● **"If you are suffering, it must be because of some unconfessed sin in your life."**

It might be! Sin does have consequences and God does discipline his beloved children (Hebrews 12:7-11). But God brings suffering into our lives for his own purposes, which are always loving and good—so it may not (and usually doesn't) have any link with our sinfulness.

The ultimate example of this is Jesus himself. He was perfect in every way—he never sinned—and yet God chose for his Son to be arrested, tortured and killed. In Acts 2, Peter explains that this was all part of God's plan: "This Jesus, delivered up according to the definite plan and foreknowledge of God, you crucified and killed by the hands of lawless men" (Acts 2:23).

- **"It's amazing how you keep going, even in such pain. I wish I had your faith."**

If we are able to stand under suffering, it's not because of anything special about us or our faith. The "amazing" element is God, not us. He is the one who gives us the strength to endure. And everyone has faith—but we place our faith in different things or people. What matters is what (or who) our faith is in.

What are some of the things we do in our church family that are unhelpful and discouraging for people who are suffering?

Sadly, your group will probably find it easy to think of examples of unhelpful and discouraging behavior! They may include avoiding the person who is suffering because we don't know what to say to them, telling someone it's their own fault, saying that someone should just pull themselves together (they would if they could), implying that someone will be healed if they just pray hard enough, or never teaching people that suffering is normal for Christians.

How do your answers show how to be helpful and supportive instead?

Take some of the examples from the previous question and use them to come up with ideas for helping and supporting those who are struggling.

Pray

"Suffering is unbearable if you aren't certain that God is for you and with you." (Tim Keller, *Walking with God through pain and suffering*)

Spend some time praising God for his love and sovereign care.

Ask him to help you to "suffer well" as you trust in his goodness.

Pray for any you know who are particularly struggling with suffering at the moment. Ask God to help you know how best to love and support them, and to point them to his goodness.

DAILY BIBLE DEVOTIONALS

This week's daily Bible devotionals walk through Romans 8, showing how we can cling on to six great gospel truths when we face times of suffering. If you know there is someone in your group who is walking through a time of trial right now, think about asking them to journal their applications and thoughts each day, and arrange to meet to talk it through with them, support them, and pray with them.

SERMONS

OPTION ONE: HABAKKUK 3:17-19

This passage is the one Vermon focuses on in the main session, which could be expanded upon in a sermon (you might choose to look at the whole of chapter 3).

OPTION TWO: HEBREWS 11:1-40

This is the passage the Bible study is based on (see next page), which could also be expanded upon in a sermon.

OPTION THREE: 1 PETER 1:3-9

This passage is not mentioned in this material, but helps us to connect gospel truths to our experience of trials, so that we rejoice through them:

- Christ's resurrection guarantees his people's dazzling, unfading inheritance (v 3-5).
- Our future hope means we can rejoice even when our present is hard (v 6).
- Our joyful hope in trials shows us that we have genuine faith, and causes us to love Christ more (v 7-9).

If one of your Sunday sermons is to be based on the theme of this session, church members will find a page to write notes on the sermon on page 131 of their Handbooks.

BIBLE STUDY

AIM: Suffering is not just a difficult question for those who reject the Christian faith. It is also problematic for those who are believers. This Bible study seeks to show that suffering is "normal" for the Christian, who might even be expected to suffer more than those who are not believers. But Christians view suffering through a very different set of lenses, which makes all the difference.

Discuss

Have you ever had a time in your Christian life when you have doubted God because of suffering? Why does the question of God's love and the existence of suffering remain one of the greatest difficulties for believing in God?

Christians can sometimes be shallow in this regard—perhaps particularly younger Christians who have not yet felt the full force of pain and suffering in the world, their family or their personal life. But bear in mind that others may be deeply hurting and struggling in this area.

READ HEBREWS 11:1-3, 32-40

¹ Now faith is the assurance of things hoped for, the conviction of things not seen. ² For by it the people of old received their commendation. ³ By faith we understand that the universe was created by the word of God, so that what is seen was not made out of things that are visible.

● *You might get your group to speed read the whole chapter from 11:1.*

In this famous passage we see how the good news of the gospel leads to people who are united in Christ and willing to follow his example of sacrificial service.

1. What picture do these verses present of what we should expect the "normal" Christian life to be like?

Encourage the group to really see the diversity of experience being talked about in these verses.

- v 33-34: God will protect and enable many believers to achieve extraordinary things for the glory of God.
- For some of us (and perhaps for only some of the time) we will be made strong to do great things for the Lord.

But there is another very real side to the experience of belonging to God:

- Torture (v 35)
- Mockery and jeering (v 36)
- Flogging and imprisonment (v 36)
- Execution by various horrible means (v 37)
- Abject poverty (v 37, 38)

Additional question (if you have time): Think about just one character from the Old or New Testament that you know well. How is their story a window into the "mixed blessing" that it is to be a follower of Christ?

Take suggestions, but if none are forthcoming, David is a good example. He was incredibly gifted, and achieved great things, but spent a long time living in a cave in the wilderness, hunted and persecuted by Saul.

- He knew the personal tragedy of losing his best friend, Jonathan.
- He fell into sin when he committed adultery with Bathsheba and murdered Uriah.
- He subsequently lost the baby son that Bathsheba had given birth to.
- He was betrayed by his son Absalom, and again cast out. He then lost his son Absalom.
- He endured a long illness as an old man.

Alternatively, for a women's group, how about Mary? She...

- bore the shame of an early pregnancy out of wedlock.
- gave birth to a wonderful son, and received many signs and gifts.
- fled to Egypt as a refugee.
- at some stage seems to have lost her husband.
- thought her son had gone mad (Mark 3:21)!
- became a believer and follower of Jesus.
- watched him die (John 19:25. "A sword will pierce through your own soul," Luke 2:35).
- became a follower of Christ and, tradition recalls, served him for many years.

2. **What enabled these believers to face both triumphs and suffering, and still maintain their trust in God (v 32-40; see also v 1)?**

   - The sure promises of God to them in the old covenant (see v 1).
   - God also was near to them, strengthening them, and giving them signs (eg: the dead back to life, v 35). But note that these signs were infrequent.
   - Their eyes were fixed on the future—not necessarily on the present.

3. **What are believers tempted to think when we face suffering?**

   - We might think that there is something wrong with us.
   - We might think that this is God punishing us because of a particular sin.
   - We might think that God has abandoned us.
   - We might be tempted to believe that God does not exist at all—that our faith is futile and wrongly founded.

How would remembering the experience of these "heroes of the faith" have helped the Hebrew Christians as they faced persecution?

   - They would realize that it is not a sign of ungodliness that we face opposition and persecution, but a sign of genuine faith.
   - They would know that, although they may experience times of great blessing as believers, suffering is an in-built part to the Christian life. In fact, it may even be unusual *not* to suffer.
   - Verse 40: these Old Testament believers trusted God's word with much less evidence of God's faithfulness than those of us living after the death and resurrection of Christ. He has something bigger in store for us...

READ HEBREWS 12:1-3

¹ Therefore, since we are surrounded by so great a cloud of witnesses, let us also lay aside every weight, and sin which clings so closely, and let us run with endurance the race that is set before us.

4. **What should we do as a result of meditating on the experiences of our Old Testament brothers and sisters?**

   - Throw off the things that encumber us—our doubts and our love for the things of this world.

- "Run with endurance" (v 1)—live as disciples of Jesus as he has commanded us.
- Remember that the normal pattern of the Christian life is: *through suffering, to glory*. This is the pattern that is revealed in full in Jesus. We must look to him.

5. Why should the example and work of Jesus Christ give us so much more confidence as we face suffering and persecution?

- Jesus went through much greater suffering than any of us—the physical pain of the cross and the emotional pain of betrayal and abandonment were a small part of it. The spiritual pain of bearing the sins of the world must have been appalling for the holy Son of God to bear. Yet because of his love for us, he endured all those things so we could be saved.
- The joy of eternity—the promise of God to him—enabled Jesus to persevere through extreme testing. The same will be true for us.
- Jesus is now seated at the right hand of the Father. We have a ruling Lord in heaven, who has suffered as we suffer. When we speak to him about suffering, he understands our pain (see Hebrews 2:18, 4:15)).
- We serve a risen Savior, who loves us enough to have died for our salvation.
- We can be sure that the God who loved us enough to send his Son to die for us will strengthen us to persevere through suffering to eternal life.

What will it mean in practice for us to look to—or fix our eyes on—Jesus (v 2)?

- The NIV translates verse 2 as: "fixing our eyes on Jesus." "Fix" implies a steady, unwavering gaze; a determination not to look away or elsewhere.
- It is Jesus we are following, so knowing his life, his teaching and his character will help us grow to be like him. In order to look to Jesus, we need to know him in and through his word—through preaching, daily devotionals and serious study of the Bible.
- It will mean taking our eyes *off* other things—ourselves, others who are helping us, or the cause of our suffering.
- It means facing suffering in the same way as Jesus faced suffering—with patience, trusting in God, and keeping focused on the big picture of what God is doing in and through this experience.

6. This is not a quick fix. Suffering and persecution can last for years. What are the twin dangers we face when suffering of any kind persists (v 3)? How can we help ourselves and each other not to succumb to these temptations?

- *Growing weary:* a long-term illness, caring for an elderly parent or a disabled child, living with the constant threat of attack for being a believer. All these things can grind us down so that we lose our focus on the glory of Jesus and the promise of eternity. We lose our joy, and then our motivation, and pretty soon we will start…
- *Becoming fainthearted:* we just lose the energy to continue being an active Christian disciple. Often we will still get along to church and go through the motions—saying the right things, even serving in other capacities. But our heart is not really in it. We become a hollow shell of a Christian, in danger of crumpling at the slightest additional burden that is placed on us.

We must keep encouraging ourselves to look to Jesus and at how wonderful and how beautiful he is. What a prize he is to look forward to! We need a constant reminder that this world is not all there is. We are looking for another country—the new creation promised to us in the gospel. So we need to keep talking about these things to each other.

Remembering heaven is something we find especially hard in the West—we have so much that heaven seems distant and unreal. So we need to discipline ourselves to keep talking up eternity, and to keep talking down our current world.

Additional question: You are talking with someone after church, and they say one of the following. How would you answer them in a way that points them to understand their suffering properly, and encourages them to walk with the Lord through it? Would you plan to do anything other than talk to them?

- "I have been battling with my depression for four years, and am just weary of trying. Why has God let this go on for so long?"
- "I lost my job last week and I just don't know what I will do—I'm just too old to get a new job, and I don't know how we will make ends meet."
- "We have been trying to have children for ten years now, and it seems that it's just not going to happen. I just feel that God is punishing me for something I did when I was younger."
- "My mother is 85 and has cancer—but I am praying that the Lord would completely heal and restore her."

It may be worthwhile splitting the group up and getting them to address different questions. Make sure that they give ideas for how some practical ongoing support is needed as well as words of comfort and encouragement.

Encourage the group not to just talk "theology" to people, but to point them to the trustworthy love and promises of God, and to the saving work and example of Jesus. Encourage people to read the Scriptures and pray with people who are distressed at their circumstances. Psalm 23 is comforting and encouraging for anyone who is suffering for whatever reason, because it points to the ultimate care of the Good Shepherd for us.

Apply

FOR YOURSELF: What do you think are the things that hinder and entangle you so that you are not running the race well? Do you think your faith is strong enough to withstand—and even flourish in the face of—physical, emotional, or relational suffering, or even persecution?

FOR YOUR CHURCH: Does your church have a culture of honesty where people can share how they are struggling—or is there a general feeling that everyone is coping and doing well? How might you be part of the way in which your church becomes a more nurturing place for people who may be suffering in silence at the moment?

Pray

FOR YOUR GROUP: Spend some time praising your Savior for his perseverance in the face of ultimate suffering. Pray for each other—that God would prepare you for the suffering that will inevitably face us all at some time.

FOR YOUR CHURCH: Pray that your preaching and conversation would encourage people to look to Jesus. Pray that those who are suffering in silence might be encouraged to seek help and support from their brothers and sisters.

FOR THE CHURCH THROUGHOUT THE WORLD: Many of our brothers and sisters worldwide are facing hostile opposition every day. Pray that those who are persecuted would continue to trust Jesus; that they would look to him, and persevere to his praise and glory.

FURTHER READING

A Christian should be an Alleluia from head to foot.
Augustine of Hippo

It is as we suffer that we show ourselves, our friends and the world that God is all in all to us. Take my money, my health, even those I love, and you have not taken what defines me. Unless you take my Jesus, you can't take my hope, my peace, my joy or my love. And you cannot take Jesus from me.
John Hindley

If our suffering unbolts our own heart to allow freer entrance by the word of God (in the words of Richard Baxter), it also unbolts our heart to allow freer flow outward of empathetic love.
D.A. Carson

Books

- *Romans 8 – 16 For You, chapters 1-3 (Tim Keller)*
- *A Place for Weakness (Michael Horton)*
- *Walking with God through Pain and Suffering (Tim Keller)*
- *Hope has its Reasons (Becky Manley Pippert)*
- *How Long, O Lord? (D.A. Carson)*
- *You Can Really Grow, chapter ten (John Hindley)*
- *Invest your Suffering (Paul Mallard)*

Online

- *Tim Keller Wants You to Suffer Well: gospelshapedchurch.org/resources361*
- *6 Pillars of a Christian View on Suffering: gospelshapedchurch.org/resources362*
- *The Beauty of Faithful Suffering: gospelshapedchurch.org/resources363*
- *The Invincible, Irrefutable Joy: gospelshapedchurch.org/resources364*
- *Jesus, You're the Greatest Joy (video): gospelshapedchurch.org/resources365*

LEADER'S REFLECTIONS

SESSION 7:

HOW TO BE THE
CHURCH
IN THE WORLD

THE CALLING OF YOUR CHURCH — TO SHINE GOD'S LIGHT
IN A DARK PLACE — IS A GREAT ONE, BUT ALSO AN
INTIMIDATING ONE. BUT GOD DOES NOT LEAVE US ALONE
IN THIS. IN THIS FINAL SESSION, WE WILL CONSIDER
HOW HIS SPIRIT IS WORKING IN, THROUGH AND AROUND
US, ENABLING US TO BE THE PEOPLE OUR FATHER HAS
CALLED US TO BE, FOR HIS GLORY AND FOR THE GOOD OF
HIS WORLD.

TALK OUTLINE

7.1 Christians are to be lights in and for a dark world. *Briefly recap the themes of sessions 2 – 6.* But the world is corrupt and our faith is weak! What do we do when we feel swamped by the size of the task? We turn to the gospel.

7.2 **KEEP IN STEP WITH THE SPIRIT** *Galatians 5:25, 17*
We are in an ongoing battle with sin, so we need to **walk by the Spirit**. This is...
- **an active, ongoing process:** To be lights for God, following him must be an active, ongoing commitment that we daily pursue. We cannot be passive consumers; it will take intentional, targeted focus to defeat sin.
- **a directional process:** Walking by the Spirit means walking in a very specific direction: toward Jesus. Ask yourself: *Am I aiming at Jesus? As a church, are we encouraging each other to become more like Jesus?* If we persist in this, God will continue to sanctify us, and Jesus will shine more brightly within us.
Give examples of the sort of active choices church members may need to make.

7.3 **FACING THE DANGERS** *Galatians 6:1-3*
How do we cope with the challenges along the road to our growing in godliness?
- **Gently restore each other when we fail:** Jesus lovingly restored Peter (John 18, 21). We should confront with gentleness those who wander from the Lord. Humbly empathize and restore, rather than condemn—it could easily be us.
- **Support each other:** Swimming against the tide is tough! We should prayerfully support one another practically, emotionally and spiritually. *Give examples of what this might look like in your church.*
- **Stay humble:** Moral pride is a great danger. Confidence in our own efforts and goodness is deadly. Focus on the gospel: we were dead in sin, but God in his grace saved us, and by his grace will lead us home. This should humble us!

SHINE!
- The challenge is great, but God is Lord of all and will work powerfully through us.
- On the day Jesus returns, we will see the success of all of our efforts for him.
- May our commitment to the gospel lead to the light of Jesus shining from our lives more clearly—for the eternal benefit of many and the praise of our Savior!

 You can download a full transcript of these talks at
WWW.GOSPELSHAPEDCHURCH.ORG/LIVING/TALKS

HOW TO BE THE CHURCH IN THE WORLD

▶ **WATCH DVD 7.1** (3 min 9 sec) **OR DELIVER TALK 7.1** (see page 146)

* *Encourage the group to make notes as they watch the DVD or listen to the talk. There is space for notes on page 135 of the Handbook.*

Discuss

Did the DVD/talk ring true for you? Do you feel swamped and inadequate to be God's light in the world? How?

Be ready to start with your own example if needed. Possible answers might include being the only Christian in a difficult work environment, seeing how enormous the social and relational needs are in your church or area, being overwhelmed by the needs of family life, or seeing how fragile, weak and resource-poor your congregation is.

▶ **WATCH DVD 7.2** (5 min 48 sec) **OR DELIVER TALK 7.2** (see page 146)

* *Encourage the group to make notes as they watch the DVD or listen to the talk. There is space for notes on page 136 of the Handbook.*

☛ **GALATIANS 5:16-17, 25**

16 But I say, walk by the Spirit, and you will not gratify the desires of the flesh. 17 For the desires of the flesh are against the Spirit, and the desires of the Spirit are against the flesh, for these are opposed to each other, to keep you from doing the things you want to do.

25 If we live by the Spirit, let us also keep in step with the Spirit.

Discuss

In verse 25, "live by the Spirit" means that we have already been brought to life by the Holy Spirit as we responded to the gospel message. So what do you think Paul is encouraging the Galatians to do when he tells them to "walk by the Spirit" and "keep in step with the Spirit"?

"Walking" and "keeping in step" both imply moving forward. This needs to happen daily, as we allow our lives to be shaped by what the Holy Spirit is urging us to do—to become more like Jesus.

"We cannot expect to be lights for God in the world if following God is not an active, ongoing commitment that we are daily pursuing." What will this look like in your life? And in the life of your church family?

Encourage the group to be specific in their answers.

For group members, this may mean general things such as daily Bible reading and prayer, but also individual issues such as how they respond to illness, the way they spend their money, or how they deal with a difficult relationship.

For the church family, it may be good to ask: "How are we encouraging each other to become more like Jesus?"

▶ WATCH DVD 7.3 (8 min 9 sec) OR DELIVER TALK 7.3 (see page 146)

* *Encourage the group to make notes as they watch the DVD or listen to the talk. There is space for notes on page 137 of the Handbook.*

👉 GALATIANS 6:1-3

¹ Brothers, if anyone is caught in any transgression, you who are spiritual should restore him in a spirit of gentleness. Keep watch on yourself, lest you too be tempted. ² Bear one another's burdens, and so fulfill the law of Christ. ³ For if anyone thinks he is something, when he is nothing, he deceives himself.

Discuss

"The church community should be the safest place to be when we fail." Why

should this be true, according to Galatians 6? Have you ever experienced restoration after failure, or seen it in your church family?

Galatians 6:1-3 shows that part of "walking in the Spirit" is that we should desire to restore people when they have failed, rather than condemn them. We know that we, too, could easily give in to temptation to sin, so we should treat others with gentleness, and look for opportunities to "bear one another's burdens."

Sadly this often doesn't happen, so you may find that no one in the group is able to give an example of experiencing restoration after failure. If this is the case, and you have time, you may want to discuss why you think church families aren't always as loving and forgiving as we should be.

"As a fellowship, we can face the things that might otherwise overwhelm and discourage us, because we don't face them alone." Can you think of some ways in which you can support others in your church family practically, emotionally and spiritually?

If you can do so without breaking confidences, try to talk about specific examples within your church family. As well as the more obvious issues such as illness or unemployment, think about how you can support people who are finding it difficult to shine for Christ in their particular situation.

Look back over your notes and journal from the previous sessions.

- **What are some of the things you have been challenged to do as an individual so that you shine more brightly (= are more like Jesus) in a dark world?**

- **What are some of the changes you could make as a church family to be a brighter, more effective light in your neighborhood?**

Many of these sessions ended with an encouragement to make some changes in how we live. Ask people to look up what they wrote at the time, as well as anything they may have written in their weekly journal section.

If you have time, ask the group how they have been getting on with living out some of the action points from earlier in the course.

Pray

👉 GALATIANS 5:22-23

> 22 But the *fruit of the Spirit is love, joy, peace, patience, kindness, goodness, faithfulness,* 23 *gentleness, self-control.*

Ask God to work in you by his Spirit so that you grow in these qualities.

Look at some of the practical things you have written on this page. Pray that you will be able to put these into practice to shine brightly in the world.

DAILY BIBLE DEVOTIONALS

The final set of devotionals looks at the church in the book of Acts, helping you see how your church can shine brightly in the world, as a devoted, prayerful, sharing, merciful, witnessing, loyal community. Do encourage your group to use this last week of studies, even if they have not done the previous ones.

SERMONS

OPTION ONE: GALATIANS 5:25 – 6:10

This passage is one that Vermon looks at in the main session and is also the focus of the Bible study (see next page), and could be expanded upon in a sermon.

OPTION TWO: MATTHEW 5:14-16

This passage is not mentioned in this session, but is the passage Vermon used as he introduced this curriculum back in Session One, and could be used to summarize all you've seen:

- The church is the light of the world as it displays the light of its Lord.
- We cannot be hidden, and must not seek to be hidden.
- As we shine Christ's light in our lives, we can expect and pray for some of those around us to come to praise God themselves.

If one of your Sunday sermons is to be based on the theme of this session, church members will find a page to write notes on the sermon on page 151 of their Handbooks.

BIBLE STUDY

AIM: In this summary session, we examine what it will mean for us to grow in Christ-likeness, as we seek to burn brighter as a light in the world.

* *On the DVD there is a vox pop of ordinary church members answering the question: "What Christ-like quality do you most struggle to grow in your life?" You might like to watch this at the start of the study to get your group thinking about the fruits of the Spirit.*

Discuss

Have you ever spoken with someone who has been "put off" Jesus because of the way they were badly treated at church or by Christians? What mistakes were made, and how could they have been corrected?

This will inevitably produce some harrowing tales of people in real need who were ignored or treated badly. The idea of this discussion is to open up the question about why churches, and particularly your own church, are not as good as they could or should be. Try to encourage people to give stories about your own church, not just others! If you have an example of a time when you did something you came to regret, share it with the group.

 READ GALATIANS 5:22 – 6:10

25 If we live by the Spirit, let us also keep in step with the Spirit...

Paul is speaking to an issue we all feel very deeply—the gap between who God has made us in Christ, and what our current lives are really like. We are not what we were, and we are not what we will be in the new creation. But now, in the "in-between times," we can still be ruled by our sinful desires, rather than by the Holy Spirit. We have been made alive by the Holy Spirit as we responded to the gospel message ("we live by the Spirit," v 25), but now we need consciously and deliberately to "keep in step with the Spirit."

1. **The phrase "keep in step with the Spirit" is a military metaphor—bringing to mind a marching army. What does this image imply about the way we should live as believers? Why does Paul mention the particular things he does in verse 26?**

A squad of soldiers marches to a particular rhythm or drum beat. Although we are all individuals with our own gifts and personalities, the Holy Spirit is urging us to be more like Jesus in our character. When we do not keep in step, not only is it disobedient, but it makes the whole squad look bad! The qualities that Paul lists in verse 26 are interesting. Ask what their opposites are, and what the common thread is between them.

- "Conceited" or prideful. The opposite is humility.
- "Provoking one another"—causing strife with other Christians. The opposite is living at peace with each other.
- "Envying one another"—perhaps for their gifts or for their possessions or situation in life. The opposite is contentment, which gives thanks to God for what we have, and for what he has given to others.

All these sins cause relational difficulties, and come from an individual's attitude that has not been transformed by the gospel of grace. We are proud, prone to division and envy each other—which will cause us to fly apart as a fellowship. But the Spirit wants us to be one in Christ.

Additional question: How, practically, can we keep in step with the Spirit?

This is an opportunity to revisit the question that was asked in the discussion as part of the main session. Keeping in step with the Spirit is the process of sanctification—so we need to keep reminding ourselves and each other of what it looks like to be truly holy, and to keep listening to sound teaching from the Scriptures. Reinforce practical ways in which we need to help each other strive to be more godly together in our daily lives. Try to be ruthlessly concrete!

2. **What are some bad ways churches might respond to an individual's personal, moral or spiritual failure? By contrast, how does the gospel urge us to deal with this problem (v 1-3)?**

The failure itself may bring the whole church into disrepute. But it may be that the greater danger is the way in which the congregation reacts to the person who has fallen. We can revert to:

- throwing them out, rather than restoring them (6:1).
- being harsh with them—rather than restoring them "gently" (v 1).

- being judgmental (see v 3).
- treating it as though it is their problem, not ours. Instead we need to bear their burdens with them (v 2).
- simply sliding down the slope after them—"lest you too be tempted" (v 1).

Note that "spiritual" here simply means people who are keeping in step with the Spirit—not some special category of Christian.

Paul outlines the right response to failure in verses 1-3. We are to restore one another gently, be vigilant against temptation in our own lives, bear the burdens of others and stay humble.

Apply

3. Which of these responses to failure have you seen happen in your church fellowship? How could you as an individual help improve on this?

Do spend time looking at the first part of this question before moving on. As individuals we can fail to keep in step with the Spirit in the way we talk about the failings of others, and the way we react to them. We can so easily gossip, or be judgmental about the failings of others, which just shows how little we understand the gospel. We are all vulnerable sinners saved by grace, and when we react wrongly to the failings of others, we show we are living by the flesh, not by the Spirit.

4. What is the principle in verses 7-8, and how does this help us in our struggle to grow in godliness?

- The principle is that everyone reaps what he sows (v 7). Paul is using the agricultural processes of reaping (harvesting) and sowing (planting).
- Whatever you sow, you will reap. Things that are sown produce a harvest, perhaps not for a long time, but the harvest of the seed will eventually come.
- If I sow to please my sinful nature—that is, I do what it wants (5:16)—then I will reap destruction. Just as farming generates produce, so does moral choice. If you give in to your sinful nature, you reap spiritual breakdown and destruction. So, for example, if I am consistently dishonest, in time my relationships will disintegrate. If I let myself grow more and more envious, I will lose all contentment and become bitter. Sin promises joy, but the harvest is all destruction.
- The right choice is to sow to please the Spirit—to obey God to please him

(rather than to save ourselves, or disobey God to seek to please ourselves). Wonderfully, as we freely live for God, we "reap eternal life" (6:8)—real life, both in terms of its quality and its quantity.

NOTE: There is a sense in which we will reap what we sow in this life in some ways. But there are other parts of Scripture where we are warned explicitly that we endanger our eternal salvation if we neglect to be obedient to Christ and grow in sanctification—see for example Matthew 7:21-23; Hebrews 2:3; Philippians 2:12.

This helps us in our struggle to grow spiritually, because it underlines the seriousness of the Christian-growth process. People can easily think: "I'm already saved, so why bother with all the effort to get holy now?" Although there is comfort and assurance that our salvation is safe and secure for the person who is growing in grace, there remain warnings for those who neglect to nurture their Christian growth.

5. **What does Paul encourage us to do in verses 9 and 10, and what does that involve?**

Do good! Note that "good" involves a value judgment. We will only know how to do good to others if we know what is truly good for them—which is informed by the will of God and the gospel as revealed in the Scriptures. So feeding the poor is good—but sharing the gospel with them is the highest good, because ultimately, it is the only thing that will raise them from their spiritual poverty.

What motivations and priorities are there for being like this?

Motivations: "In due season we will reap" (v 9). We will see fruit and benefits (in our own lives and characters, and in those around us), eventually. But just as a farmer has to wait for harvest, so we must wait for the promised reaping. Second, Christians are part of a family ("household," v 10). Believers are adopted sons of God (4:5-6)—fellow Christians are brothers and sisters. When we do good in our church fellowship, we are doing and being family.

Priorities: We are to do good to all, but especially to other Christians (6:10). The Christian life is not primarily about meetings, programs, or even conversions—

it is about doing good to the person in front of us, giving them what is best (which may be challenging or restoring them, v 1). Notice that we are to *do* good—Paul is thinking of deeds as well as words.

The "family" language is helpful here. Strong biological families tend to love each other more deeply, and look out for each other more quickly, than they do others—but without ceasing to love and support those outside the family. I am particularly keen to do what is best for my wife and children, but that does not mean I neglect to seek to do good to my neighbor or my co-worker. So it is with Christians—we are to do good first of all to our family of believers, but such an attitude and commitment will overflow to our treatment of those who are not Christians, rather than constraining it.

6. **Why is it easy for us to "grow weary of doing good"? How can we combat love fatigue?**

   - We can try to do good with the wrong motivation. If so, we will easily become weary. If we want to feel blessed by doing good, and feel tired instead, we'll get weary of doing good for others. If we are doing good to gain recognition but no one notices, we'll get weary. If we are doing it because we think we have to do so as Christians, then we'll grow resentful and stop doing it (or do it joylessly and minimally).
   - We can also become weary of serving others when we take on too much, perhaps because we feel the burden of the need but do not trust in the sovereignty and power of God enough.
   - If, on the other hand, we do good to please God and because we truly want to love others, then we won't grow weary of it, however tiring, unnoticed or difficult burden-bearing becomes.
   - Notice that we serve the world, and adorn the gospel, by being both a loving community *and* by being that loving community in the world, when God's gospel-goodness to us spills over into how we treat everyone.

Review

YOURSELF: Look back together over what we have looked at in these seven sessions. What did you find particularly challenging? How can you maintain your own growth in godliness as an individual and as part of the congregation?

YOUR CHURCH: What does your church struggle most with, do you think? Growing in a holy, gracious and vibrant Christian life; or showing that life attractively and compellingly to a world that is hungry for authentic, truthful and loving relationships?

Pray

FOR YOUR GROUP: Ask the Lord to help you be honest about your own weaknesses and failures with each other, and that you would deal with each other gently and lovingly.

FOR YOUR CHURCH: Pray that your leaders would help you grow in godliness and in effective witness in the world.

FURTHER READING

Will God ever ask you to do something you are not able to do? The answer is yes—all the time! It must be that way, for God's glory and kingdom. If we function according to our ability alone, we get the glory; if we function according to the power of the Spirit with us, God gets the glory. He wants to reveal himself to a watching world.
Henry Blackaby

Those in whom the Spirit comes to live are God's new temple. They are, individually and corporately, the place where heaven and earth meet.
N.T. Wright

The fruit of the Spirit is a gift of God, and only he can produce it. They who bear it know as little about it as the tree knows of its fruit. They know only the power of him on whom their life depends.
Dietrich Bonhoeffer

Books

- *Galatians For You, chapters 11 to 13 (Tim Keller)*
- *What is the Mission of the Church? (Kevin DeYoung & Brad Gilbert)*
- *Who on Earth is the Holy Spirit? (Tim Chester)*
- *Keep in Step with the Spirit (J.I. Packer)*
- *The Prodigal Church (Jared Wilson)*

Online

- Encourage One Another: Giving Grace with Your Words: gospelshapedchurch.org/resources371
- The Litmus Test of Genuine Christianity: gospelshapedchurch.org/resources372
- Has Authenticity Trumped Holiness? gospelshapedchurch.org/resources373
- Can I Grow in Holiness Without the Local Church? (video) gospelshapedchurch.org/resources374

LEADER'S REFLECTIONS

GOSPEL SHAPED

CHURCH

The Complete Series

LET THE POWER OF THE GOSPEL SHAPE FOUR OTHER CRITICAL AREAS IN THE LIFE OF YOUR CHURCH

"WE WANT CHURCHES CALLED INTO EXISTENCE BY THE GOSPEL TO BE SHAPED BY THE GOSPEL IN THEIR EVERYDAY LIFE."

DON CARSON AND TIM KELLER

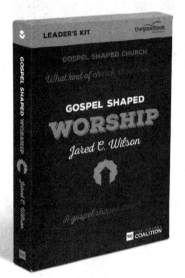

GOSPEL SHAPED
WORSHIP

Christians are people who have discovered that the one true object of our worship is the God who has revealed himself in and through Jesus Christ.

But what exactly is worship? What should we be doing when we meet together for "church" on Sundays? And how does that connect with what we do the rest of the week?

This seven-week whole-church curriculum explores what it means to be a worshiping community. As we search the Scriptures together, we will discover that true worship must encompass the whole of life. This engaging and flexible resource will challenge us to worship God every day of the week, with all our heart, mind, soul and strength.

Written and presented by **JARED C. WILSON**
Jared is Director of Communications at Midwestern Seminary and College in Kansas City, and a prolific author. He is married to Becky and has two daughters.

WWW.GOSPELSHAPEDCHURCH.ORG/WORSHIP

GOSPEL SHAPED
OUTREACH

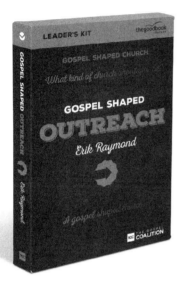

Many Christians are nervous about telling someone else about Jesus. The nine sessions in this curriculum don't offer quick fixes or evangelism "gimmicks." But by continually pointing us back to the gospel, they will give us the proper motivation to work together as a church to share the gospel message with those who are lost without Christ.

As you work through the material, you will discover that God's mission of salvation in the world is also your mission; and that he is inviting you into the privilege of praying and working to advance his kingdom among your family, friends, neighbors, co-workers and community.

Gospel Shaped Church is a new curriculum from The Gospel Coalition that will help whole congregations pause and think slowly, carefully and prayerfully about the kind of church they are called to be.

Written and presented by **ERIK RAYMOND**
Erik is the Preaching Pastor at Emmaus Bible Church in Omaha, Nebraska. He is married to Christie and has six children.

WWW.GOSPELSHAPEDCHURCH.ORG/OUTREACH

GOSPEL SHAPED
WORK

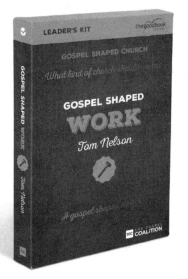

Many Christians experience a troubling disconnect between their everyday work and what they live and work for as a believer in Jesus. How should the gospel shape my view of life on an assembly line, or change my work as a teacher, artist, nurse, home-maker or gardener?

Gospel Shaped Work explores over eight sessions how the gospel changes the way we view our work in the world—and how a church should equip its members to serve God in their everyday vocations, and relate to the wider world of work and culture.

These engaging and practical sessions are designed to reveal the Bible's all-encompassing vision for our daily lives, and our engagement with culture as a redeemed community. They will provoke a fresh discussion in your church about how the gospel of Christ impacts every area of life in our world.

Written and presented by **TOM NELSON**
Tom is the Senior Pastor of Christ Community Church in Kansas City, and a council member of The Gospel Coalition. He is married to Liz and has two grown children.

WWW.GOSPELSHAPEDCHURCH.ORG/WORK

"THESE RESOURCES GIVE SPACE TO CONSIDER WHAT A GENUINE EXPRESSION OF A GOSPEL-SHAPED CHURCH LOOKS LIKE FOR YOU IN THE PLACE GOD HAS PUT YOU, AND WITH THE PEOPLE HE HAS GATHERED INTO FELLOWSHIP WITH YOU."

DON CARSON AND TIM KELLER

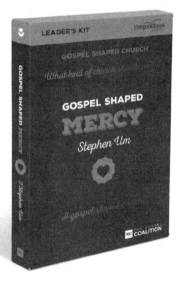

GOSPEL SHAPED
MERCY

The gospel is all about justice and mercy: the just punishment of God falling on his Son, Jesus, so that he can have mercy on me, a sinner.

But many churches have avoided following through on the Bible's clear teaching on working for justice and mercy in the wider world. They fear that it is a distraction from the primary task of gospel preaching.

This *Gospel Shaped Mercy* module explores how individual Christians and whole churches can and should be engaged in the relief of poverty, hunger and injustice in a way that adorns the gospel of grace.

Written and presented by **STEPHEN UM**
Stephen is Senior Minister of Citylife Church in Boston, MA, and is a council member of The Gospel Coalition.

WWW.GOSPELSHAPEDCHURCH.ORG/MERCY

MORE RESOURCES
TO HELP SHAPE YOUR
LIVING

Let **the gospel** frame the way you **think and feel**

This workbook shows how ordinary Christians can live the life that God calls us to. By focusing our attention on the gospel, everyday problems familiar to Christians everywhere can be transformed as the cross of Christ becomes the motive and measure of everything we do. *Gospel Centered Life* shows how every Christian can follow the way of the cross as they embrace the liberating grace of God in Christ.

STEVE TIMMIS is Global Director for Acts 29

TIM CHESTER is Director of the Porterbrook Seminary

WWW.THEGOODBOOK.COM/GCL

LIVE**DIFFERENT**

" I HAVE COME THAT THEY MAY HAVE LIFE AND HAVE IT TO THE FULL. "

JOHN 10:10

"As I was reading John's book, I found myself in conversations with some of the very people it addresses—people who serve, but who are growing weary of serving. It was a joy to recommend the book to them."

Tim Challies
BLOGGER & AUTHOR

This warm and pastoral book by Tim Lane helps readers to see when godly concern turns into sinful worry, and how Scripture can be used to cast those worries upon the Lord. You will discover how to replace anxiety with peace in your life, freeing you to live life to the full.

TIM LANE is President of the Institute for Pastoral Care, USA, and co-author of *How People Change*

WWW.THEGOODBOOK.COM/LD

LIVE | GROW | KNOW

Live with Christ, Grow in Christ, Know more of Christ.

"These studies by Becky Pippert are clear and accessible, yet substantial and thoughtful explorations of how to be grounded and grow in Christian faith. They evidence years of experience working with people at all stages of belief and skepticism. I highly recommend them."

Tim Keller

PART 1
live

Explores what the Christian life is like.

Ever got to the end of running an evangelistic course and wondered: What next?

LiveGrowKnow is a brand new series from globally renowned speaker Rebecca Manley Pippert, designed to help people continue their journey from enquirer to disciple to mature believer.

Part 1, Live, consists of five DVD-based sessions and is the perfect follow-up to an evangelistic course or event, or for anyone who wants to explore the Christian life more deeply.

REBECCA MANLEY PIPPERT
Globally renowned speaker and author of
Out of the Saltshaker

PART **2**
grow

Explores how we
mature as Christians.

I'm a Christian… what next?
These studies show what God's plan for
our lives is, and how we can get going
and get growing in the Christian life.

For groups who have done the LIVE
course, GROW is the follow-up; it also
works perfectly as a stand-alone course
for groups wishing to think about how
to grow in a real and exciting way.
Handbook and DVD available.

PART **3**
know

Looks at core
doctrines of the faith.

WWW.THEGOODBOOK.COM/LGK

thegoodbook
COMPANY
Opening up the Bible

At The Good Book Company, we are dedicated to helping Christians and local churches grow. We believe that God's growth process always starts with hearing clearly what he has said to us through his timeless word—the Bible.

Ever since we opened our doors in 1991, we have been striving to produce resources that honor God in the way the Bible is used. We have grown to become an international provider of user-friendly resources to the Christian community, with believers of all backgrounds and denominations using our Bible studies, books, evangelistic resources, DVD-based courses and training events.

We want to equip ordinary Christians to live for Christ day by day, and churches to grow in their knowledge of God, their love for one another, and the effectiveness of their outreach.

Call us for a discussion of your needs or visit one of our local websites for more information on the resources and services we provide.

North America: www.thegoodbook.com
UK & Europe: www.thegoodbook.co.uk
Australia: www.thegoodbook.com.au
New Zealand: www.thegoodbook.co.nz

North America: 866 244 2165
UK & Europe: 0333 123 0880
Australia: (02) 6100 4211
New Zealand (+64) 3 343 2463